SMALL
$\mathscr{P}$ATCHWORK QUILTS

PIPPA ABRAHAMS

Garnet
PUBLISHING

INTRODUCTION

The origin of the word quilt comes from the French word *cuilte*, which is itself derived from the Latin *culcita* meaning mattress or cushion. A quilt is a bed-coverlet made of padding enclosed between two layers of cloth and kept in place by cross lines of stitching.

There is a resurgence of interest in the craft of patchwork and quiltmaking. It draws on the traditions and techniques of many cultures and traditions. Most designs appearing in today's quilts are based on ancient tribal, folk and applied art patterns that appear throughout the globe. Similar recurring geometric patterns are to be found in all ancient civilisations and form part of the shared heritage of humankind.

This common inheritance, combined with the enthusiasm and creativity of American quilt makers, is responsible for the popularity of the craft today. As societies defer to the power of technology, we increasingly turn to the arts and crafts to remind us of our humanity. The craft of patchwork and quiltmaking transcends political, and cultural divisions. It provides an absorbing interest that links peoples everywhere. It exists both as a legitimate art form and also as a functional, decorative skill that enriches the lives and environments of the people who make and treasure them.

The making of a quilt celebrates our existence as individuals. The mention of the word 'quilt' conjures up the image of a bed, awakening ritual memories of our passage through life. Indeed my first quilt was made to celebrate the birth of my friend Dee's daughter, Cara Slattery. It was a small coverlet made up of hexagonal shapes, clumsily and inexpertly pieced together by oversewing the sides. That small gift changed my life. Through it I discovered the joy of working with textiles and creating something decorative. It opened a door that has led to an enduring enchantment with the craft and to an entirely unexpected career as a maker and teacher.

Two important factors made certain that Cara's quilt was completed. First it was small and secondly it was made especially for her. Traditionally apprentices learnt their craft by studying the work of master craftsmen, and by making small-scale articles to hone their skills. In the same way, the objective of this book is to offer small projects suitable for beginners to the craft and for those who appreciate fine craftsmanship and wish to brush up on the basics.

In the past few decades quiltmaking has developed and changed enormously. New materials and equipment are constantly being developed that revolutionise the way quilts are made. As well as basic construction techniques, I have described contemporary methods that will speed up the quiltmaking process. Full-size templates and quilting designs are provided for both traditional and speed techniques.

Every quilt has its own special problems to overcome and pleasures to be enjoyed. The small quilts in this book are offered as an opportunity to enjoy the construction and finishing methods described. My hope is that in the process you will develop sufficient confidence in your skills and techniques to go on to make your own unique heirloom quilt.

Today quilts are no longer being made purely for functional and decorative reasons. They hang on the walls of art galleries and museums. Artists, taking images and artifacts from their immediate experience and surroundings, use the quilt form as a medium for political and personal statements. Their work comments on uncomfortable social issues and mirrors the experience and concerns of contemporary society. However the majority of contemporary quilts created are historically based on the classic block patterns. They are joyfully made to give pleasure to loved ones, to decorate homes, and to raise money for charitable causes. That a tension should exist between the artist and the populist maker is natural. Such tension can be used to spur us on in our endeavour to perfect and develop the form we prefer. We should have every confidence that what is of value in the quilt art movement will survive together with the best of the classical. Inevitably, the best of both will become the traditional quilt forms of tomorrow.

Pippa Abrahams

Pippa Abrahams, London, 1995.

Important note: a ¼-inch seam allowance is used on all projects in this book, unless otherwise stated.

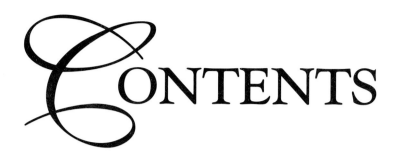

CONTENTS

FAST PATCH SAMPLER

The speed techniques used to make this three-block sampler require no templates. They include: strip piecing, fast triangles and an easy method for making wild goose units.

QUILT SIZE
25 x 59 inches

MATERIALS
(based on 42-inch fabric width)

Blocks: Assorted fat quarters (18 x 22 inches) or fabric scraps in light, medium and dark colours

Setting triangles: 1½ yards

Accent border and binding: ¾ yard

Outer border: 1¼ yards

Backing: 1¼ yards

2-oz polyester wadding: 1¼ yards

1 MAKING THE WILD GOOSE CHASE BLOCK

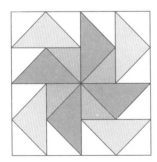

Block size: 12 inches

This block can be made entirely from rectangles and squares cut from a collection of four contrasting fabrics cut into fat quarters (18 x 22 inches).

CUTTING

1 Cut two 3½-inch strips of a light-coloured fabric. Slice into twelve squares 3½ x 3½ inches.

2 Cut one 3½-inch strip of the first medium-coloured fabric. Slice into four squares 3½ x 3½ inches.

3 Cut four 3½-inch strips of the second medium-coloured fabric. Slice into four rectangles 3½ x 6½ inches.

4 Cut four 3½-inch strips of the dark fabric. Slice into four rectangles 3½ x 6½ inches.

PREPARING THE UNITS

1 On the wrong side of the 3½-inch squares lightly mark a diagonal line (corner to corner).

2 Mark a second line ½ inch to one side of the diagonal.

3 Place a marked 3½-inch square on a 3½ x 6½-inch rectangle with right sides together. Sew two seams along the marked lines.

4 Cut between the seams, as shown. The smaller half-square triangle unit produced will not be used here (save for another project). Fold back the larger triangle from the rectangle. Press.

5 Place a second marked square on the adjacent side of the rectangle. Sew the two seams on the marked lines as illustrated.

6 Cut between the two seams as in step 4. Fold back the large triangle to complete the unit. Press.

7 Make four Unit As.

8 Make four Unit Bs.

BLOCK CONSTRUCTION

1 Join the As and Bs to make four Unit Cs.

2 Join Cs to make two Unit Ds.

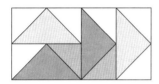

3 Join two Unit Ds to complete the block, as shown.

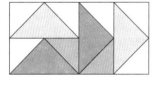

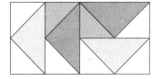

2 MAKING THE NINE PATCH BLOCK

Block size: 12 inches

One of the simplest blocks to make, Nine Patch is often used for a first quilt and looks stunning made with a collection of recycled scraps set together with a harmonising background fabric. The cutting guide here is given for two contrasting fabrics.

CUTTING GUIDE

1 Cut one 4½-inch strip of light fabric and slice into four squares 4½ x 4½ inches.
2 Cut one 2½-inch strip of light fabric from selvedge to selvedge.
3 Cut one 4½-inch square from the contrasting fabric.
4 Cut one 2½-inch strip of contrast fabric from selvedge to selvedge.

PREPARING THE UNITS

1 Join the two 2½-inch strips right sides together. Reduce the stitch

length on the sewing machine and join the strips using a ¼-inch seam allowance along the long sides.

2 Press the closed seam to lock the stitches, then open out and press the seam allowance toward the darker fabric.

3 Using a rotary ruler, straighten the end. Then slice into eight segments 2½ inches wide.

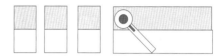

4 Join them as shown below to make four unit As.

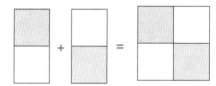

BLOCK CONSTRUCTION

1 Lay out the units and squares on a flat surface and piece together in rows.

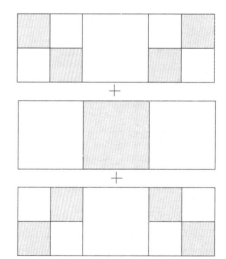

2 Join the rows together to complete the block (illustration overleaf).

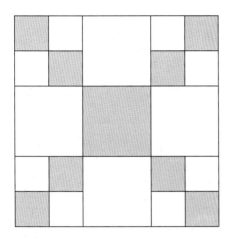

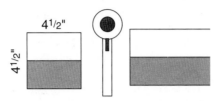

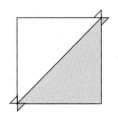

allowance. Press to lock the stitches. Open out and press the seam allowance towards the darker fabric.

3 Straighten the end with a rotary cutter and slice off four squares 4½ x 4½ inches.

4½"

4½"

and grid lines. Press to lock the stitches. Open out the resulting half-square triangle units and press the seam allowance towards the darker fabric. Trim off the ears that appear at the corners (see illustration below).

3 MAKING THE CHURN DASH VARIATION BLOCK

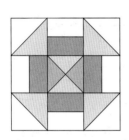

Block size 12 inches
This variation uses four contrasting fabrics and is made up of several modular units that appear constantly in patchwork. They are: half-square rectangles, half-square triangles and quarter-square triangles. Instructions are given for each unit separately.

CUTTING
AND CONSTRUCTION
Half-square rectangles
(4 inch finished size)
Half-square rectangle units are squares composed of two rectangles of equal dimensions. They are easily made using the following strip piecing method:

1 Cut one 2½-inch strip of fabric 1 and one from fabric 4, cutting from selvedge to selvedge.
2 Place the fabrics right sides together. Reduce the stitch length on the sewing machine and sew the strips together along the long edges, using a ¼-inch seam

Half-square triangle units
(4 inch finished size)
Half-square triangle units are squares composed of two right-angled triangles. The long diagonal edge or hypotenuse of the triangles lies on the bias grain of the fabric. They are speedily constructed by drafting a grid either onto a paper guide or directly onto the fabric (the method used here). The grid size is determined by adding ⅛ inch to the dimension of the finished size of the unit square. In this case the finished size of the square unit is 4 inches so the grid size will be 4⅛ inches.

1 Cut one rectangle of fabric 1, 5½ x 10½ inches. Cut a second rectangle of the same dimensions from fabric 2.
2 On the wrong side of the lighter fabric, draft two adjoining 4⅛-inch squares. Draw a diagonal line in each square as illustrated. The seam lines are drawn ¼ inch either side of the diagonals.

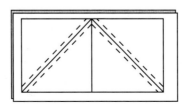

3 Place the two rectangles right sides together and sew on the marked seam lines. Cut on the diagonal

Quarter-square triangle units
(4 inch finished size)
Quarter-square triangle units contain four triangles. The long side or hypotenuse of a quarter-square triangle lies on the straight grain of the fabric. The centre square of the Churn Dash block contains four such triangles. As with the half-square triangles a grid is drafted to produce the triangles. The grid size is determined by adding 1¼ inches to the finished size of the square unit containing the triangles.

1 Cut one 6½-inch square from fabric 1 and one 6½-inch square from fabric 3.
2 Draft a 5¼-inch square on the wrong side of the lighter fabric. Draw diagonal lines from each corner.
3 Mark sewing lines a quarter of an inch either side of one diagonal only. See illustration.

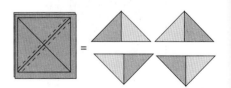

4 Reduce the stitch length on the sewing machine and sew the seams on the marked sewing lines. Cut on each of the remaining lines and press to lock the stitches. Four pairs of triangles are produced from

this method. Sew them together as illustrated.

PIECING THE BLOCK

1 Lay out the completed units and piece together in rows.

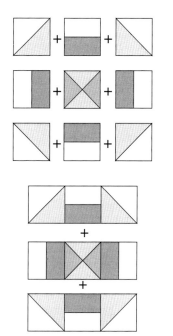

2 Sew the rows together to complete the blocks.

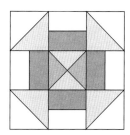

SETTING TRIANGLES FOR 12-INCH FINISHED BLOCKS

The triangles used to complete the diagonal set of the blocks are larger versions of the half-square and quarter-square units that have just been completed. They are commonly

known as setting triangles. Before calculating the grid size it is necessary to know what the diagonal measurement of the finished block is. To find the diagonal measurement of a square, multiply the finished size of the square by 1.4142 and round up to the nearest ⅛ inch. For example, the diagonal measurement of a 12-inch square is calculated as follows:

12 x 1.4142 = 16.9704 inches
(or 17 inches)

Quarter-square setting triangles for 12-inch finished blocks
To determine the size of a square that will produce the four setting triangles required add 1¼ inches to the diagonal measurement of the finished size of the block. It has already been established that the diagonal measurement of the block is 17 inches. Therefore 17 + 1¼ = 18¼ inches.

Either make a paper pattern this size or draft the 18¼-inch square directly on to the wrong side of the fabric. Cut in four across each diagonal to obtain the four setting triangles.

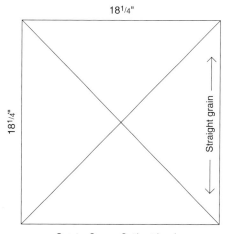

Quarter-Square Setting triangles for 12-inch finished blocks.

Half-square corner triangles for 12-inch finished blocks
One square will produce two of these corner triangles. The formula for determining the size of the square to draft is to add ⅞ inch to half the diagonal measurement of the finished square.

The diagonal measurement is 17 inches. Half of 17 is 8½.
The size of square to draft therefore is 8½ + ⅞ = 9⅜.

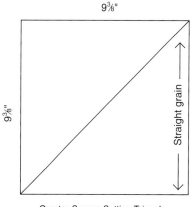

Quarter-Square Setting Triangles for 12-inch finished blocks

Draft two 9⅜-inch squares on the wrong side of the fabric. Cut in half through the diagonal to obtain two corner triangles from each square.

SETTING THE THREE BLOCKS TOGETHER

1 Refer to the illustration overleaf and lay out the blocks and setting triangles in the order they will be pieced.
2 Sew together in three diagonal rows as illustrated oveleaf. Next join the rows together.
3 Add the two corner triangles to complete the central panel of the sampler.

PIECING THE BORDERS
The inner border
Make two accent-coloured strips 1 x 51½ inches and two strips 1 x 17½ inches. Attach the long strips first to either side of the panel and then add the shorter strips to the top and the bottom, using a ¼-inch seam allowance. Be careful to keep the seam line straight. The slightest wobble will show on an accent strip as narrow as this.

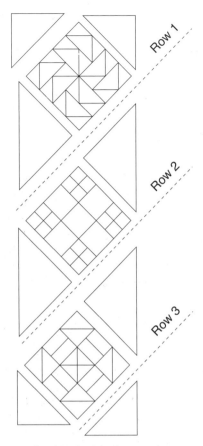

Setting the blocks together

The borders

The mitred border

1 From the outer border fabric cut two strips 3½ x 63 inches and two strips 3½ x 28 inches.

2 Press the quilt-top and mark a dot ¼ inch in from each of the four corners. Measure the length of the quilt through the centre to confirm that the actual measurement is 52½ inches.

3 Fold one of the long border strips in half crossways and press lightly to mark the centre. From the centre, measure out half the length determined in step 2, i.e. half of 52½ inches is 26¼ inches (adjust to fit the length you measured). Mark this length with a pin. Measure the same distance on the other side of the centre crease, and again mark with a pin.

4 Mark a dot on the seam line ¼ inch in from the pins to indicate the start and finish of the seam.

Crease, pin and mark the second long border strip in the same way.

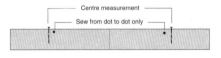

5 Measure across the centre of the quilt and confirm that the measurement is 17½ inches.

6 Fold one of the shorter border strips in half and press lightly to mark the centre. Measure out from the centre half the measurement determined in step 5, i.e. half of 17½ inches is 8¾ inches. Mark with a pin. Measure out the same distance from the other side of the centre crease and again mark with a pin. Mark the seam dots on each strip as in step 4.

7 Starting at the centre and with the border strip on top, pin baste the

border to the quilt top. Match the pins to the edge of the top and pin through the seam dots to secure the border. Complete the pin basting, easing where required to make the quilt top fit the border strip.

8 Attach each border strip to the quilt top, stopping and starting each seam at the seam dots.

Using a rotary ruler with a 45° angle, mark the mitred seam on the wrong side of the fabric. Refer to the Skill Basics section for detailed guidance (page 56).

QUILTING AND FINISHING

Press the quilt top, and tidy up any stray threads that may show through the fabric.

On a flat surface, smooth out the backing with the wrong side facing upwards. Secure with masking tape or with cloth clamps to prevent it from shifting. Unfold the wadding and pat it into place using a wooden rule to smooth it gently over the backing. Centre the quilt top right side up, over the wadding. Gently smooth out any ripples using the ruler and baste the sandwich together. See Skill Basics section, Basting the Sandwich for further details.

Quilt the design: suggested outline quilting for the blocks is illustrated in the Skill Basics section (page 57).

HANGING SLEEVE AND BINDING

Attach the hanging sleeve and continuous binding (a detailed explanation is in the Skill Basics section, page 58).

Nine Patch

A simple and effective design set off by a strip-pieced, mitred border. Practise rotary cutting and strip piecing to make the quilt in double-quick time. The quilt illustrated is made in two colours. It will look striking made with brightly coloured scraps on a darker background.

QUILT SIZE 23 x 29 inches
BLOCK SIZE 3 inches

MATERIALS
(based on 42-inch fabric width)
Light fabric: 1 yard
Dark fabric: 1 yard

CUTTING
Inner border
From the light fabric, cut two strips 1½ x 32 inches and two strips 1½ x 26 inches.

Middle border
From the dark fabric, cut two strips 1½ x 32 inches and two strips 1½ x 26 inches.

Outer border
From the light fabric, cut two strips 2½ x 32 inches and two strips 2½ x 26 inches.

Blocks
1   From the light fabric, cut four 1½-inch strips.
2   From the light fabric, cut two 3½-inch strips. Slice into 17 squares of 3½ inches.
3   From the dark fabric, cut five 1½-inch strips.

Backing and wadding
1   From the backing fabric cut a rectangle 27 x 33 inches.
2   From the wadding cut a rectangle 27 x 33 inches.

CONSTRUCTION
Strip piecing the blocks
1   Make two of band A by sewing together two dark and one light coloured strips (see below). Press seam allowance towards the darker material.

Make 2 band A

2   Straighten the edge. Cut 36

rectangles of 1½ x 3½ inches from the bands.

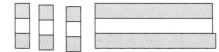

3   Make one band B by sewing two light coloured strips to one dark coloured one (see below). Press the seam allowances towards the darker fabric.

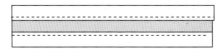

4   Square off the ends of each combination strip using either a set square or a wide rotary ruler marked with a cross grid. Cut 18 rectangles of 1½ x 3½ inches from band B.

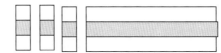

5   Lay out the rectangles as illustrated below and make the 18 Nine Patch blocks.

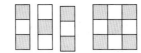

Piecing the top
1   Make four of row A.

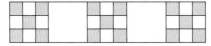

2   Make three of row B.

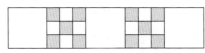

3   Sew the rows together as shown right.

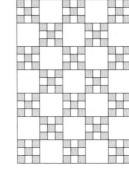

Piecing the borders
The simplest and most effective way to make the mitred border is to first join the border strips together as illustrated. Then mitre the corners in the

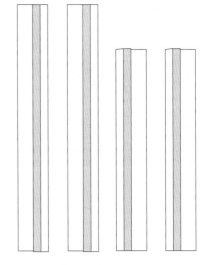

usual way by sewing up to a point ¼ inch from the corner, and back-tacking at that point. See Skill Basics section for detailed instructions on how to attach a mitred border (page 56).

QUILTING AND FINISHING
Press the quilt top, and tidy up any stray threads that may show through the fabric.

On a flat surface, smooth out the backing with the wrong side facing upwards. Secure with masking tape or with cloth clamps to prevent it from shifting. Use a wooden rule to smooth the wadding gently over the backing. Centre the quilt top right side up, over the wadding. Smooth out any ripples using the ruler and baste the sandwich together. See Skill Basics section (page 56) for further details.

Quilt a simple grid design over the surface. Apply continuous French binding (see Skill Basics, page 58) to complete the quilt.

SAILBOATS

An easy-to-make quilt for sailing enthusiasts. It is made of three 9-inch sailing boat blocks separated by two sashing strips, and framed with a narrow inner border surrounded by a wider, mitred border.

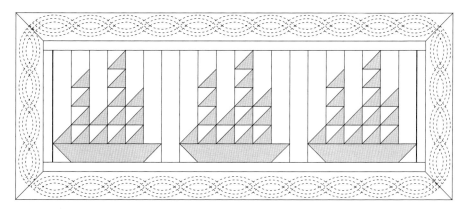

QUILT SIZE 15 x 36 inches
BLOCK SIZE 9 inches

MAKING TEMPLATES

See the illustration (right) to identify the templates required for the block and the sashing strip. The full-size template patterns are provided. Note that the half-square triangle units not marked in the illustration with a template number are cut using the fast triangle guide (page 13) to speed up the construction process.

MATERIALS

(based on 42-inch fabric width)
Background fabric: 1¼ yards
Sailboat fabric: ¼ yard
Binding fabric: ¼ yard
Backing fabric: ⅝ yard
2-oz polyester wadding: ⅝ yard

CUTTING

From the background fabric
1　Template 1: cut six triangles.
2　Template 3: cut three.
3　Template 4: cut three.
4　Template 5: cut three.
5　Template 6: cut three.
6　Template 7: cut three.
7　Template 8: cut two.
8　Fast triangle guide: cut three rectangles 9 x 6 inches.
9　Inner side borders: cut two strips 1¼ x 9¼ inches.
10　Inner top and bottom borders: cut two strips 1¼ x 32 inches.
11　Outer side borders: cut two strips 2¾ x 18 inches.
12　Outer top and bottom border: cut two strips 2¾ x 39 inches.

From the sailboat fabric
1　Fast triangle guide: cut three rectangles 9 x 6 inches.
2　Template 1: cut twelve.
3　Template 2: cut three.

From the binding fabric
Cut three 2½-inch strips from selvedge to selvedge.

From the backing fabric
Cut rectangle 19 x 40 inches.

From the wadding
Cut rectangle 19 x 40 inches.

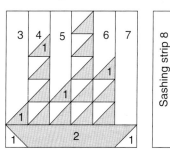

Templates required

CONSTRUCTION

Half-square triangle units (see page 60)
1　Make three copies of the fast triangle guide given on page 13. Cut around the paper guide, leaving space around the outside of the marked grid.
2　Place one background and one sailboat fabric rectangle right sides together. If necessary pin to secure. Place a paper guide on top of the rectangles and secure with masking tape. With a short stitch length, start sewing at the top corner. Following the direction of the arrows sew along the dotted line. By pivoting at the corners it

is possible to complete the sewing with just one seam. Cut along the solid lines using rotary cutting equipment. Remove the paper guide by gripping the seam firmly between index finger and thumb. Fold the seam allowance portion down and pull gently but firmly away from the stitches, still holding the seam to avoid stretching it. The larger piece of paper should peel off easily. Press the seam allowances towards the darker fabric and trim the 'ears' that appear. Use 11 half-square triangle units for each boat.

Piecing the top

1   The piecing of the block is quite straightforward. See illustration below for the construction sequence. Press the seam allowances towards the darker fabric as you go.

2   Complete the three blocks. Attach a sashing strip to two of the blocks and then join all three into a row (see illustration, facing page).

3   Attach the short inner border strips to either side.

4   Next attach the long inner border strips to the top and the bottom. Press.

To attach the mitred border refer to the Skill Basics section, page 56.

QUILTING AND FINISHING

Press, and tidy up any stray threads that may show through the fabric.

A full-sized cable quilting pattern is given. Using greaseproof or tracing paper, trace off the design and make a template for marking the design onto the outer border.

On a flat surface, smooth out the backing with the wrong side facing upwards. Secure with masking tape or with cloth clamps to prevent it from shifting. Unfold the wadding and pat it into place using a wooden rule to smooth it gently over the backing. Centre the quilt top right side up, over the wadding. Gently smooth out any ripples using the ruler and baste the sandwich together. See Skill Basics section, Basting the Sandwich for further details (page 56).

A simple way to complete the quilting is by outline quilting around the sailboats, with extra quilting between the blocks and around the inner border. Finally bind the quilt.

HANGING SLEEVE AND BINDING

Attach the hanging sleeve and continuous binding (a detailed explanation is to be found in the Skill Basics section, page 56).

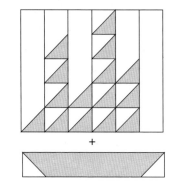

Construction sequence for sailboat block

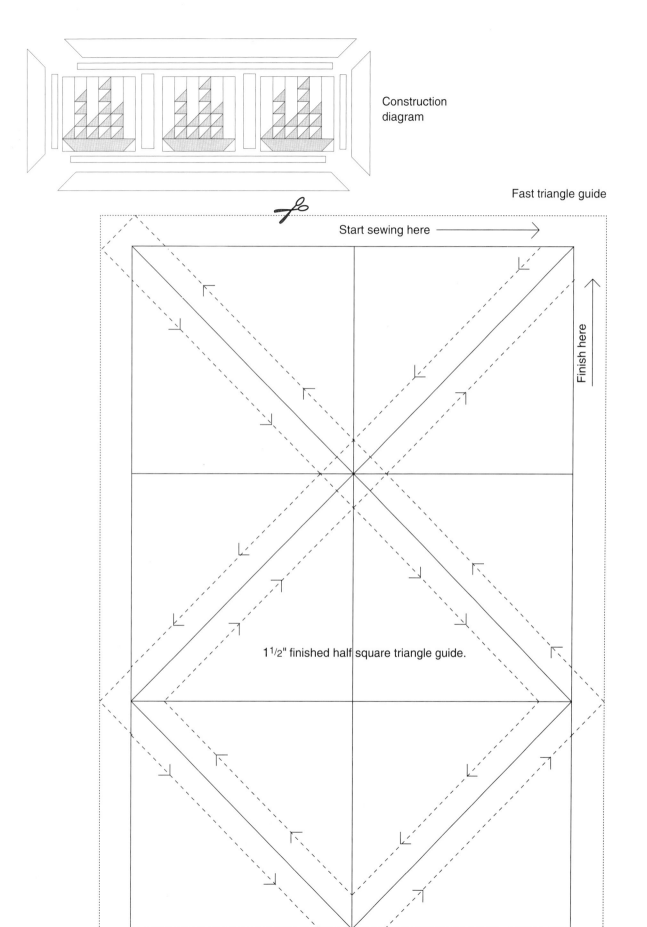

Construction
diagram

Fast triangle guide

Start sewing here ⟶

Finish here

$1\frac{1}{2}$" finished half square triangle guide.

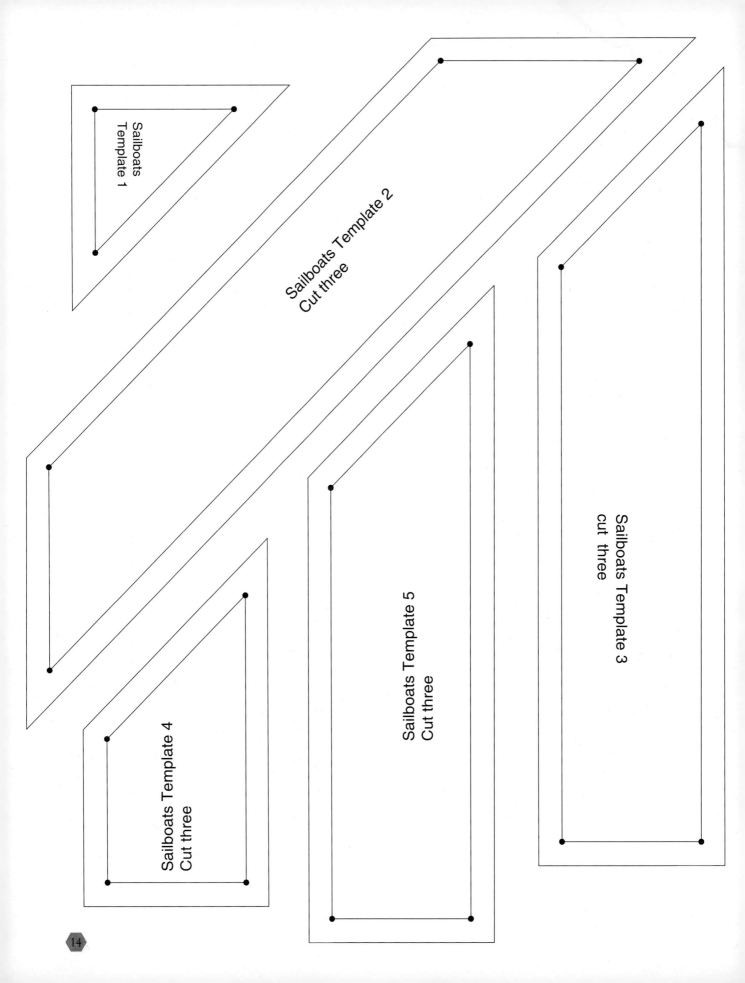

Sailboats
Template 1

Sailboats Template 2
Cut three

Sailboats Template 3
cut three

Sailboats Template 5
Cut three

Sailboats Template 4
Cut three

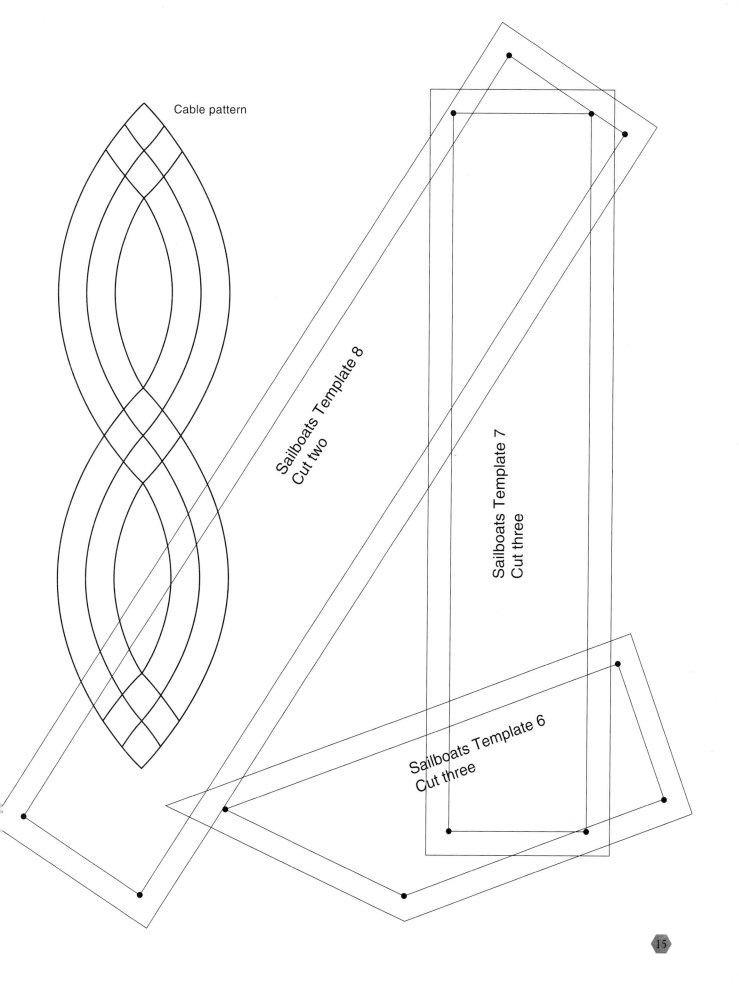

Cable pattern

Sailboats Template 8
Cut two

Sailboats Template 7
Cut three

Sailboats Template 6
Cut three

TRIPLE RAIL FENCE

A simple, strip-pieced quilt that uses colour values to outline the design. Three fabrics of well contrasted light, medium and dark colours are required.

QUILT SIZE 39 x 48 inches
BLOCK SIZE 4½ inches

MATERIALS
Light patterned fabrics generally have a cream or white background. The medium values are the most difficult to determine. If you are uncertain whether you have sufficient value contrast in the fabrics you are considering, try taping a sample of each fabric to a sheet of A4 paper and take a black-and-white photocopy. The resulting grey-scale copy will clearly show whether or not you have sufficient contrast.

(Based on 42-inch fabric width):
Light fabric: 1½ yards
Medium fabric: ½ yard
Dark fabric: 1½ yards
Backing fabric: 1½ yards
2-oz polyester wadding: 1½ yards

CUTTING
From the light fabric
1   Blocks: cut seven strips 2 x 42 inches.

2 Inner Border A: cut two strips 2 x 36½ inches.

3 Inner Border B: cut two strips 2 x 30½ inches.

4 Binding: cut five strips 2½ x 42 inches from selvedge to selvedge.

From the medium fabric
Blocks: cut seven strips 2 x 42 inches.

From the dark fabric
1 Blocks: cut seven strips 2 x 42 inches.

2 Outer Border A: cut two strips 5 x 39½ inches.

3 Outer Border B: cut two strips 5 x 39½ inches.

From the backing fabric
Cut rectangle 42 x 52 inches.

From the wadding
Cut rectangle 42 x 52 inches.

CONSTRUCTION
Piecing the blocks

1 Using an accurate ¼-inch seam allowance, sew one light, one medium and one dark strip together. On some machines, the action of the feed dogs causes the strips to curl. To counter this problem start each seam from opposite ends.

Test the accuracy of the seam allowance by checking that the measurement across the combined strips is 5 inches. Adjust the seam

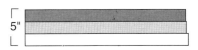

allowance if necessary. Make a total of six of these combination strips. Press the seam allowances towards the darkest fabric.

2 Square off the ends of each combination strip using either a set square or a wide rotary ruler marked with a cross grid.

3 Cut 48 squares 5 x 5 inches from the combination strips. As you progress with the cutting you

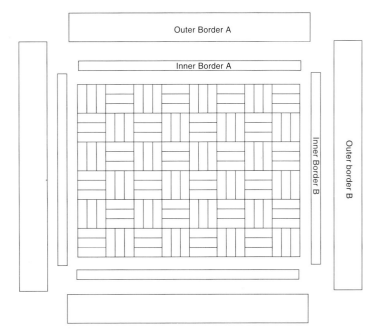

may find that occasionally you need to straighten off the end of the strip before cutting the next square.

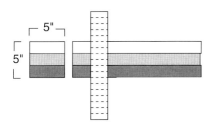

4 Sew six blocks together to form a row as illustrated (row A). Make four of these row As.

5 Sew six blocks together to form a row as illustrated (row B). Make four of these row Bs.

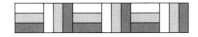

6 Refer to the illustration on page 16 and join the completed rows together to form the central panel of the quilt top. Press seam allowances towards the darkest fabric.

Adding the borders
Refer to the illustration above. For more detailed instructions see the Skill Basics section (page 54).

1 Sew Inner Border A strips to either side of the quilt top.

2 Sew Inner Border B strips to the top and bottom

3 Attach Outer Border A strips to either side

4 Attach Outer Border B strips to the top and bottom.

QUILTING AND FINISHING
Press the quilt top and tidy up any stray threads that may show through the fabric.

On a flat surface, smooth out the lining with the wrong side facing upwards. Secure with masking tape or with cloth clamps to prevent it from shifting. Unfold the wadding and pat it into place using a wooden rule to smooth it gently over the surface. Centre the quilt top right side up, over the wadding. Gently smooth out any ripples using the ruler and baste the sandwich together. See Skill Basics, page 56 for details.

Outline quilt (see photograph) then remove the basting thread. Attach binding to complete. Refer to Skill Basics section for instructions.

OHIO STAR

A simple setting with straight borders and corner squares. Scaled up this would make a good project for a bed quilt. Instructions are given for rotary cutting and for fast piecing of the quarter-square triangle units that make the stars twinkle on the surface. Full-size templates are provided for those who prefer traditional cutting, marking and sewing methods.

QUILT SIZE 51 x 39 inches
BLOCK SIZE 6 inches
PIECED BLOCKS 18
PLAIN BLOCKS 17

MATERIALS
(based on 42-inch fabric width)

Light fabric: 2½ yards
Dark fabric: 1⅝ yards
Backing fabric: 1½ yards
2-oz polyester wadding: 1½ yards

CUTTING

Inner border
1 From light fabric cut two strips 42 x 1½ inches.
2 From dark fabric cut four 1½-inch squares.

Outer border
1 From dark fabric cut two strips 44½ x 4 inches and two strips 32½ x 4 inches.
2 From light fabric cut four 4-inch squares.

Plain blocks
From light fabric, either use rotary cutting equipment to cut three 6½-inch strips from selvedge to selvedge, then slice the strips into 17 6½-inch squares. OR use Template 3 to mark and cut the 17 squares.

Ohio blocks
Choose one of three possible methods for cutting and making the triangles:
EITHER Use rotary cutting equipment to cut three 3¼-inch strips from selvedge to selvedge from both the light and the dark fabric. Slice the strips into 36 3¼-inch light and 36 dark squares. Slice each square twice diagonally to yield 144 dark and 144 light quarter square triangles.
OR use Template 2 to mark and cut the 144 light and 144 dark triangles.
OR use the following speed construction method to produce the quarter-square triangle units required for the block (see illustration, top right).

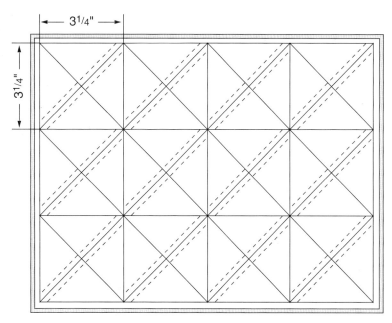

← 3¼" →

3¼"

Quarter-Square Triangle Grid
Sew on the dotted lines, cut on the solid lines.

1 Cut three 15 x 12-inch rectangles of light fabric and three of dark.
2 On the wrong side of the lighter fabric draft a 3¼-inch grid.
3 Draw a diagonal line through each square as illustrated above.
4 Mark the sewing lines (dotted in illustration) ¼ inch to either side of the diagonals. See pages 61–62 for quarter-square triangle units.
5 For the squares, use rotary equipment to cut (selvedge to selvedge) five 2½-inch strips of dark and two 2½-inch strips of light material. Slice the strips into 2½-inch squares: 72 dark and 18 light. OR cut the squares using Template 1.

Continuous French binding
Cut five 2½-inch strips from selvedge to selvedge and join together. (See Skill Basics, page 58.)

Backing and wadding
From both fabrics cut a rectangle 42 x 54 inches.

CONSTRUCTION
Piecing the blocks
1 Make 144 of unit A.

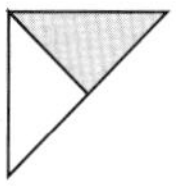

2 Join two unit As to make each unit B (make 72 of unit B).

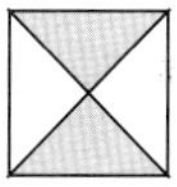

3 Using half the unit Bs and dark squares, make 36 of unit C.

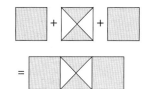

4 Using the remaining unit Bs, make 18 of unit D.

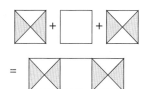

5 Lay out the C and D units as illustrated and join together to make 18 blocks.

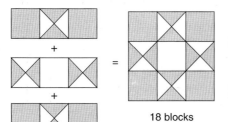

18 blocks

Piecing the top

1 Arrange the pieced and plain blocks in rows as shown (right) and piece together in rows.

2 Set the rows together in sequence to complete the pieced section of the quilt.

Borders (illustration below right)

1 Sew the inner border strips to the long sides.

2 Sew the small corner blocks to either end of the remaining inner border strips and attach them to the top and bottom of the quilt.

3 Sew the outer border strips to the long sides.

4 Sew the corner blocks to either end of the remaining outer border strips and attach them to the top and bottom of the quilt.

QUILTING AND FINISHING

Press the quilt top, and tidy up any stray threads.

A full-size Feathered Wreath quilting design is given opposite. Trace off and mark onto the fabric (see Skill Basics, page 51).

Baste together the quilt top, wadding and backing. See Skill Basics section, Basting the Sandwich for further details (page 56).

Quilt the design. Finish the edge with continuous French binding (see Skill Basics, page 58).

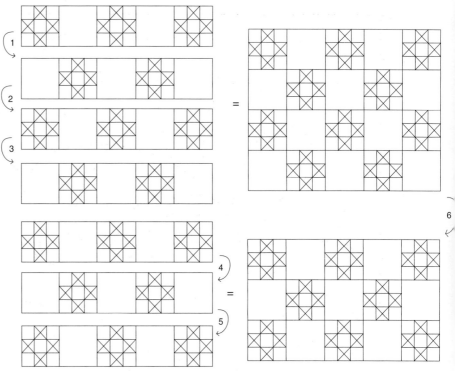

Piecing the top sequence

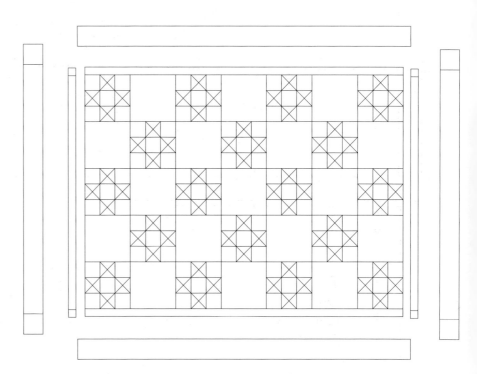

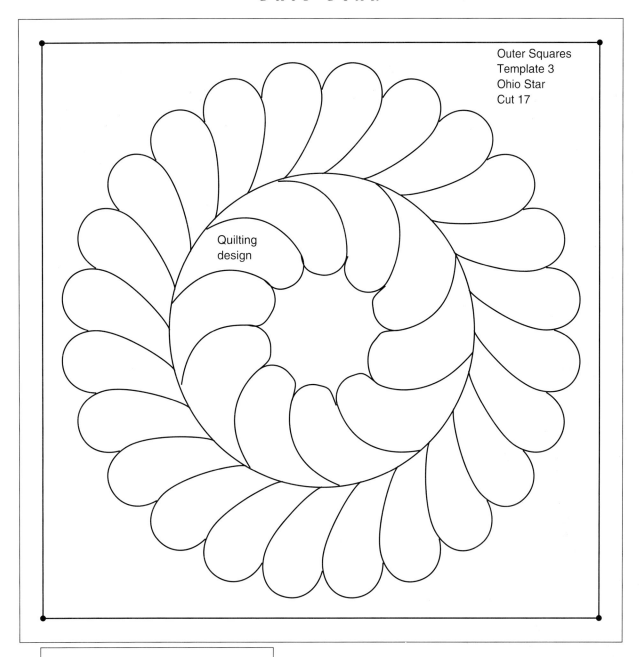

Outer Squares
Template 3
Ohio Star
Cut 17

Quilting
design

Template 1
Ohio Star
Cut 72 dk
Cut 18 light

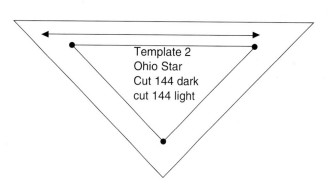

Template 2
Ohio Star
Cut 144 dark
cut 144 light

CHINESE COINS

This is a very versatile and easy to make quilt, made up of three pieced columns of scrap fabrics separated by two bars of solid fabric. An accent-coloured inner border and an outer border of dark fabric pieced with contrast setting squares are used to frame the quilt. This quilt can be made in several ways - scrap fabrics will make a rich variety of 'coins', or you could use a series of graduated colour values against a dark backgound for a dramatic splash of colour.

QUILT SIZE 25 x 31 inches

MATERIALS
(based on 42-inch fabric width)
Scrap fabrics: ¼ yard
Dark fabric: ¾ yard
Accent fabric: ½ yard
Backing fabric: 1 yard
2-oz polyester wadding: 1 yard

CUTTING
From the scrap fabrics
Coins: cut 63 rectangles 3½ x 1½ inches.

From the dark fabric
1 Bars: cut two rectangles 21½ x 3½ inches.
2 Outer Border A: cut two rectangles 25½ x 4½ inches.
3 Outer Border B: cut two rectangles 23½ x 4½ inches.
4 Inner Border: cut four 1½-inch squares.

From the accent fabric
1 Inner Border A: cut two rectangles: 21½ x 1½ inches.

2 Inner Border B: cut two rectangles 15½ x 1½ inches.
3 Outer Border: cut four squares 4½ x 4½ inches.
4 Binding: cut three strips 2½ inches from selvedge to selvedge.

From the backing fabric
Cut one rectangle 29 x 36 inches.

From the wadding
Cut one rectangle 29 x 36 inches.

Note: border dimensions do not include working allowance. Refer to Skill Basics section, Measuring and Cutting Borders (page 54).

CONSTRUCTION
Piecing the top
1 Sew the 3½ x 1½-inch rectangles into three columns. Each column is made up of 21 patches sewn together on the long edge, using a ¼-inch seam allowance. Press. Check that the measurement lengthwise through the centre of each column measures 21½ x 3½ inches, and adjust if necessary.

2 Refer to the illustration below and attach the two bar strips. Press.

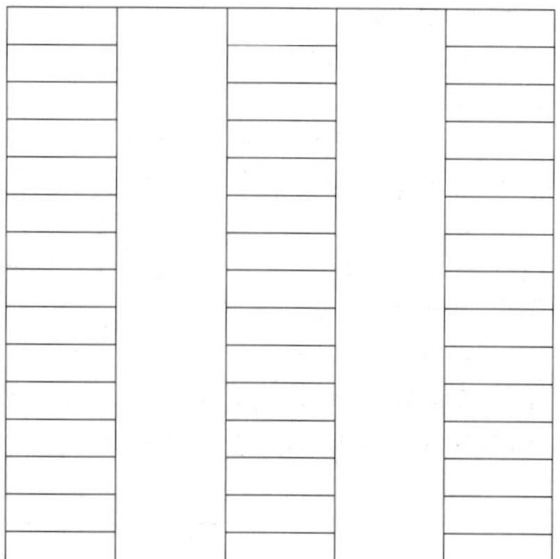

Adding the borders

1 Attach Inner Border A strips to either side of the quilt top and press.

2 Sew a small, dark-coloured square to either end of Inner Border B strips. Press and attach to the quilt top.

3 Attach Outer Border A strips and press. Sew accent-coloured squares to either end of Outer Border B strips. Press.

QUILTING AND FINISHING

Press the quilt top and tidy up any stray threads. Press the backing fabric.

The border interlocking circles and the feathered wreath patterns are given full size overleaf. Trace off the design and mark onto the quilt top (see Skill Basics, page 51).

On a flat surface, smooth out the lining with the wrong side facing upwards. Secure with masking tape or with cloth clamps to prevent it from shifting. Unfold the wadding and pat it into place using a wooden rule to smooth it gently over the surface. Centre the quilt top right side up, over the wadding. Gently smooth out any ripples using the ruler and baste the sandwich together. See Skill Basics section, Basting the Sandwich (page 56) for further details.

To finish the quilt attach continuous French binding. See Skill Basics section for detailed instructions (page 58).

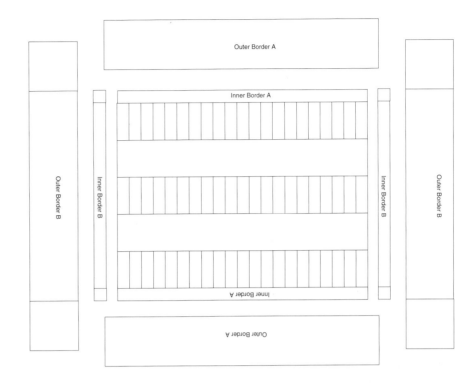

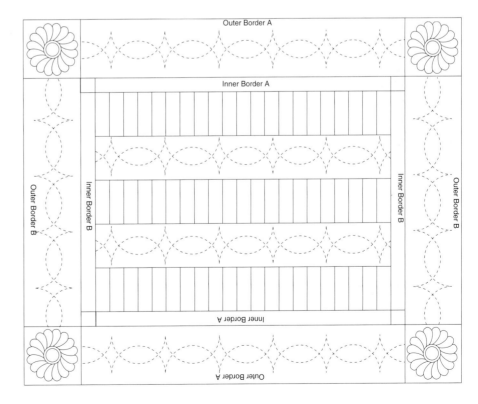

$\mathscr{A}$MISH SHADOWS

The blocks used in the quilt are made up of two half-square triangles set together on the diagonal. One half is made up of coloured strips of fabric set against the black 'shadow' of the facing half-square triangle. The striped triangles on the top and bottom edges of the central medallion are mirror images of each other. Three borders frame the central panel: an inner border, a pieced middle border made from the same combination strips that are used in the blocks, and a wide outer border. Full-size patterns for the templates are provided.

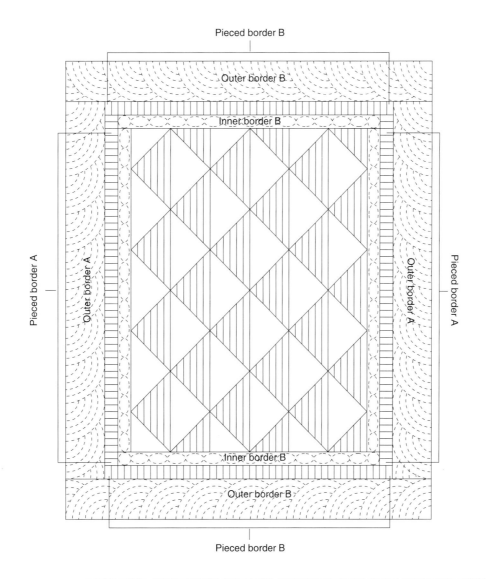

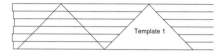

QUILT SIZE 51 x 42 inches
BLOCK SIZE 6⅛ inches

MATERIALS
(based on 42-inch fabric width)
Six coloured fabrics: ⅛ yard each
Black fabric: 2 yards
Backing fabric: 1¼ yards
2-oz polyester wadding: 1¼ yards

CUTTING
From the six coloured fabrics
Using rotary cutting equipment cut six strips 1¼ inches wide from selvedge to selvedge from each fabric, making a total of 36 cut strips.

From the black fabric
1 Large triangles: using Template 1 with the short sides aligned with the straight grain, mark and cut 21 large half-square triangles.
2 Small triangles: using Template 2 with short sides aligned to straight grain mark and cut six triangles.
3 Inner Border A: cut two strips 36½ x 2 inches.
4 Inner Border B: cut two strips 30½ x 2 inches.
5 Outer Border A: cut two strips 42½ x 5 inches.
6 Outer Border B: cut two strips 42½ x 5 inches.
7 Binding: cut five strips, each 2½ inches wide from selvedge to selvedge.

From the backing fabric
Cut one rectangle 55 x 45 inches.

From the wadding
Cut one rectangle 55 x 45 inches.

Note: border dimensions do not include working allowance. Refer to Skill Basics section, Measuring and Cutting Borders (page 54).

CONSTRUCTION
Piecing the blocks
1 Sew the cut 1¼-inch strips together to form a six-colour strip

combination. Make six of these units. Press the seam allowances in one direction.
2 Place Template 1 right side up with the long edge aligned against the bottom of a combination strip

and mark the half-square triangle. One strip combination will yield seven triangles. Cut a total of 21 triangles using the rotary cutter. The remaining strip combinations will be used to piece the striped middle border.
3 Sew a black half-square triangle to each strip-coloured triangle to complete the 18 blocks required.

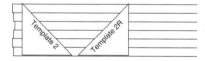

4 Place Template 2 right sides up, with the short edge aligned along the straight grain of the remaining

strip combinations, and mark three triangles. Flip the template to its reverse side to mark the three mirror image triangles that are required.

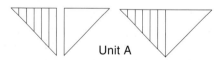
Unit A

5 Make two Unit A triangles (sew a black to a strip-coloured triangle, as shown).
6 Then make two Unit B triangles, as shown.

Unit B
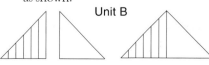

7 Lay out the completed blocks with perimeter triangles and add the remaining small corner triangles (see illustration on facing page). Pick up the diagonal rows with setting triangles on each end and sew together one row at a time. Then sew the completed rows together.

Borders
(Refer to Skill Basics section for further instructions, and see illustration on page 25.)
1 Sew an Inner Border A strip to each long side of the block panel. Then sew Inner Border B to the shorter top and bottom edges.
2 Each Pieced Border A consists of eight segments cut 2 inches wide from the remaining combination strips. Sew each of the eight segments together along their 2-inch sides to form a long strip. It will be slightly too long, so remove two coloured rectangles from either end of the strip to give a

2"

finished measurement of 39 x 1½ inches. Make two of these strips, and attach one to either side of the quilt top.
3 Each Pieced Border B consists of nine segments cut 2 inches wide from the combination strips. Sew each of the nine segments together along the 2-inch sides to form a long strip. It will be slightly too long, so remove one coloured rectangle from either end to give a finished measurement of 33 x 1½ inches. Make two of these strips and attach to the top and bottom of the quilt top.
4 Attach a plain Outer Border A strip to either side of the quilt. Complete the quilt top by

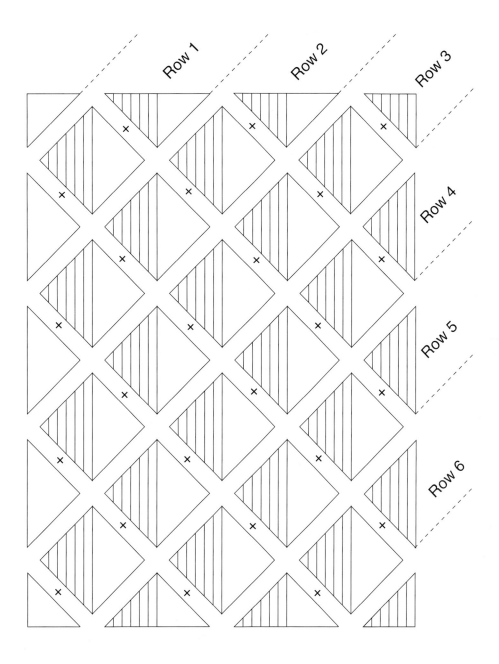

attaching Outer Border B strips to the top and bottom.

QUILTING AND FINISHING

Press the quilt top. Tidy up any stray threads that may show through the fabric.

The wave quilting design on the Outer Border is given full size overleaf. Mark it onto the quilt top with a suitable marker (see Skill Basics, page 51).

On a flat surface, smooth out the lining with the wrong side facing upwards. Secure with masking tape or with cloth clamps to prevent it from shifting. Unfold the wadding and pat it into place using a wooden rule to smooth it gently over the surface. Centre the quilt top right side up, over the wadding. Gently smooth out any ripples using the ruler and baste the sandwich together. See Skill Basics section, Basting the Sandwich (page 56) for further details.

Quilt, and attach continuous French binding. See Skill Basics section (page 58) for further details.

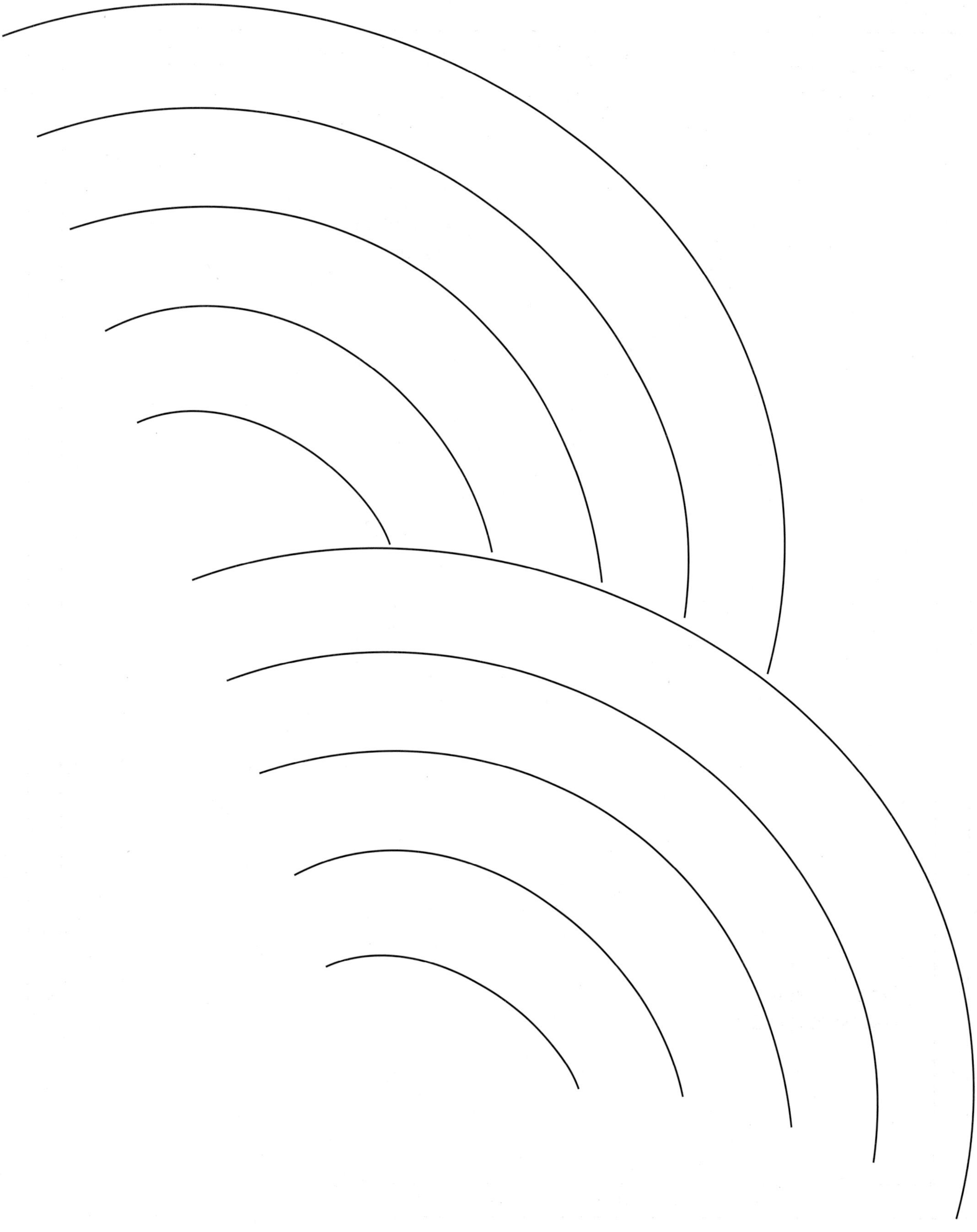

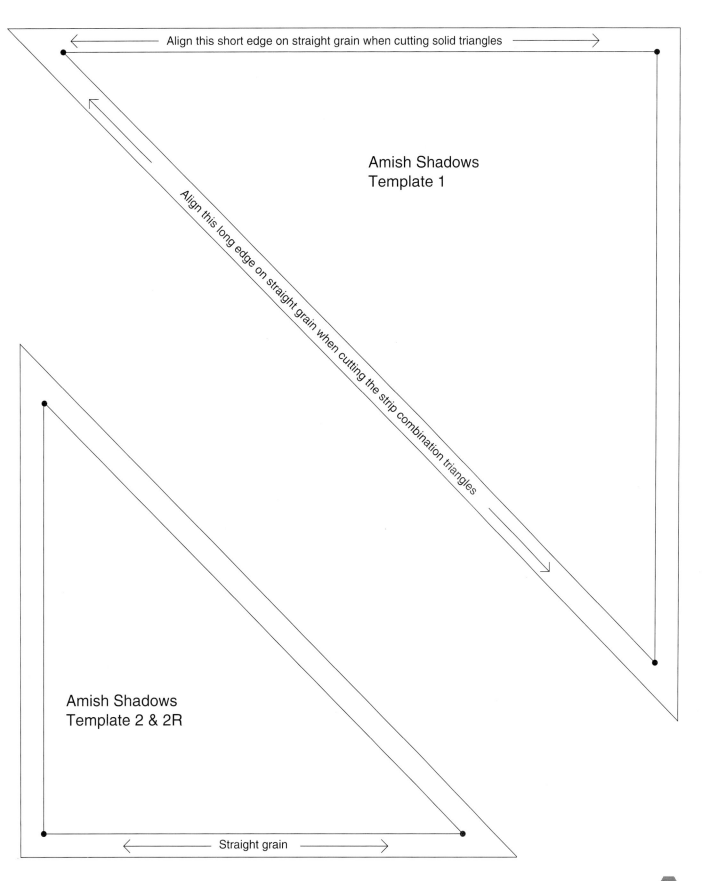

Align this short edge on straight grain when cutting solid triangles

Amish Shadows
Template 1

Align this long edge on straight grain when cutting the strip combination triangles

Amish Shadows
Template 2 & 2R

Straight grain

PINWHEEL SQUARES

This is a two-block quilt. Small Pinwheel blocks are set side by side with Square in a Square. Try making it with Amish bright colours set against a dark background. Or use just two contrasting colours, as illustrated.

QUILT SIZE 38 x 38 inches
BLOCK SIZE 4 inches
PINWHEEL BLOCKS: 29
SQUARE IN A SQUARE BLOCKS: 24

MATERIALS
(based on 42-inch fabric width)

Light fabric: 1⅝ yards
Dark fabric: 2 yards
Backing fabric: 1¼ yards
2-oz polyester wadding: 1¼ yards

CUTTING
Inner border
1 From light fabric, cut two strips 30½ x 1½ inches.
2 From light fabric, cut two strips 28½ x 1½ inches.

Outer border
From dark fabric cut four strips 30½ x 4½ inches.

Binding
From light fabric, cut four 2½-inch strips from selvedge to selvedge.

Blocks
1 From dark fabric cut five 2⅞-inch strips. Slice into 58 squares. Slice the squares in half diagonally for 116 triangles (Template 1).
2 From light fabric cut eight 2⅞-inch strips. Slice into 106 squares. Slice in half diagonally for 212 triangles (Template 1).
3 From the dark fabric cut three 4¾-inch strips. Align the grainline on Template 2 with the straight grain and cut into 24 squares.

Backing and wadding
From both the backing fabric and the wadding cut a square measuring 41 x 41 inches.

CONSTRUCTION
Piecing the blocks
(use a ¼-inch seam throughout)
1 Make 116 of Unit A.
2 Join to make 58 of Unit B.

Unit A   Unit B

3 Take two Unit Bs, and rotate one by 180°.

Rotated 180°

4 Sew together, carefully matching the centre points (Unit C). Make 29 of these Pinwheel blocks.

Unit C

5 Sew light-coloured triangles to each bias edge of each of the dark squares (Unit D). Make 24, to complete the piecing of the blocks.

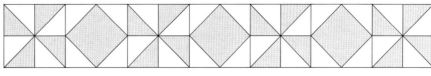

Row 1

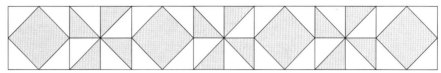

Row 2

PIECING THE TOP

Arrange the blocks in rows.
1 Make four of Row 1.
2 Make three of Row 2.
3 Sew the rows together in alternate sequence to complete the pieced section of the quilt.

ATTACHING THE BORDERS

1 Sew the shorter inner borders to either side of the pieced section.
2 Attach the remaining inner borders to the other two sides.
3 Attach an outer border to either side (illustration next column).
4 Sew a Pinwheel block to each end of the remaining border strips. Add these strips to either side to complete the quilt top.

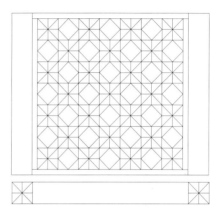

Attaching the borders

QUILTING AND FINISHING

Press the quilt top, and tidy up any stray threads that may show through the fabric.

On a flat surface, smooth out the backing with the wrong side facing upwards. Secure with masking tape or with cloth clamps to prevent it from shifting. Unfold the wadding and pat it into place using a wooden rule to smooth it gently over the backing. Centre the quilt top right side up, over the wadding. Gently smooth out any ripples using the ruler and baste the sandwich together. See Skill Basics section, Basting the Sandwich (page 56) for further details.

Quilt the sandwich. Finish the edge with continuous French binding (see page 58).

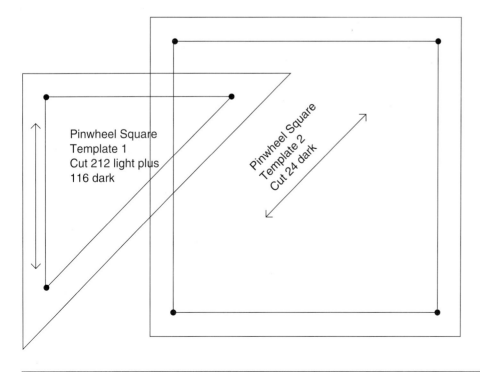

Unit D

Pinwheel Square
Template 1
Cut 212 light plus
116 dark

Pinwheel Square
Template 2
Cut 24 dark

DOUBLE WEDDING RING

The Double Wedding Ring design looks trickier than it is to piece. The secret of getting the curves and points to match lies in the preparation of the templates and the marking and cutting of the pattern pieces. The templates should be pierced at the junction of the seam lines, to enable a pencil dot to be transferred through to the wrong side of the fabric patch. An awl or a large tapestry needle can be used to make the hole. Balance marks are registered in the same way along the curved edges of the background melon and centre pieces. It is important to transfer these marks accurately to the fabric.

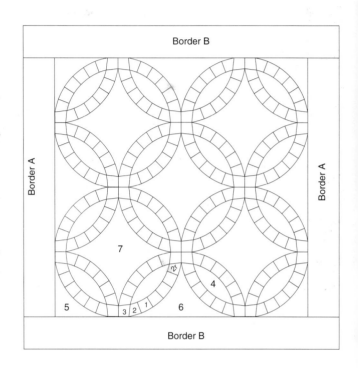

QUILT SIZE 35 x 35 inches
RING SIZE 14 inches

MATERIALS
Choose scrap fabrics for the rings, with accent colours at the four post patches that will harmonize the colour scheme. A pale tint of the accent colour works well as the background. (Based on 42-inch fabric width):
Scrap fabrics: ¼ yard
Accent fabric: ¼ yard
Background fabric: 2 yards
Backing fabric: 1⅛ yards
2-oz polyester wadding: 1⅛ yards

CUTTING
From the scrap fabrics
1 Template 1: cut 128.

2 Template 2 and 2r: mark and cut 32. Flip the template over and mark another 32 reversed. Make sure that the dots are marked on the wrong side of the patch edge which is to be sewn to the post patches to be cut from Template 3.

From the accent fabric
Template 3: mark and cut 32 (post patches). Make sure that the seam dots are marked on the wrong side of the fabric.

From the background fabric
1 Template 4 (melon): cut 16. Transfer balance marks and seam dots to wrong side of fabric.
2 Template 5 (corner pieces): cut four. Mark seam dots and balance marks.
3 Template 6: cut four. Mark seam

dots and balance marks.
4 Template 7 (centre pieces): cut five. Mark seam dots and balance marks.
5 Binding: cut four strips 2½ x 42 inches across the grain from selvedge to selvedge.

From the backing fabric
Cut rectangle 39 x 39 inches.

From the wadding
Cut rectangle 39 x 39 inches.

Note: border dimensions do not include working allowance. Refer to Skill Basics section, Measuring and Cutting Borders (page 54).

CONSTRUCTION
Piecing the blocks
1 Join four Template 1 pieces together to make Unit A. Make 32

of these units. Press the seams in one direction.

Unit A

2 Attach one piece each of Template 2 and 2r to either end of the Unit As to make 32 Unit Bs. Press the seams in one direction.

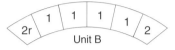

Unit B

3 Attach the accent-coloured post patches to either end of half of the Unit Bs to make 16 Unit Cs.

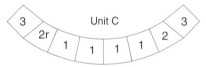

Unit C

4 Attach the background melon shapes: place a unit B and a melon piece right sides together with the melon piece on top. Match the dots and balance marks, and pin together. Start to sew at the dot

Match the dots

mark on the end point of the melon piece. Stop at the dot matching with '2r'. Do not sew beyond the dots. Press seams towards the melon piece.

5 To complete the melon unit a 3-step seam is required. Step A: with the melon section on top of Unit C, match the balance marks and dots. Sew from dot to dot along the side of the melon, starting at and stopping at the dots at each end. Step B: starting at the outer

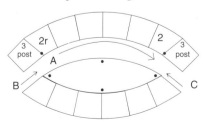

edge of a post piece sew towards the melon piece and stop at the dot. C: complete Unit D by joining the second post piece in

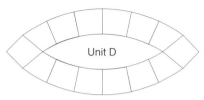

Unit D

the same way. Press seams towards the melon piece. Make 16 Unit Ds.

6 Place a centre background piece on top of a Unit D. Match the balance marks, pin and sew from dot to dot. Repeat the sequence until four Unit Ds are attached to complete the Wedding Ring. Make four of these units.

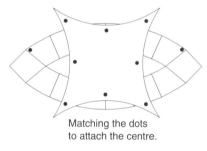

Matching the dots to attach the centre.

7 Refer to the illustration overleaf. Attach the centre background piece in the same way as described in step 6, above. Because it will be necessary to start and stop sewing at the dots on the background pieces, the seam that joins the post sections

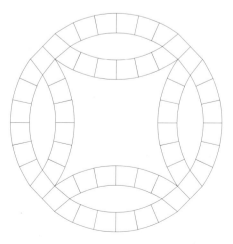

will complete the piecing of the top. Continue to piece until all the sections are joined.

The completed Wedding Ring block is shown clearly in this cushion

BORDERS

The quilt has a simple butted border. (For more detailed instructions see Skill Basics section, page 54.)

Attach Border A strip to either side of the quilt top and then Border B strips to top and bottom.

QUILTING AND FINISHING

Press the quilt top, and tidy up any stray threads that may show through the fabric.

Mark the quilting design with a suitable marker.

On a flat surface, smooth out the lining with the wrong side facing upwards. Secure with masking tape or with cloth clamps to prevent it from shifting. Unfold the wadding and pat it into place using a wooden rule to smooth it gently over the surface. Centre the quilt top right side up, over the wadding. Gently smooth out any ripples using the ruler and baste the sandwich together. See Skill Basics section, Basting the Sandwich (page 56) for further details.

Quilt the sandwich, then bind to complete it (see page 58).

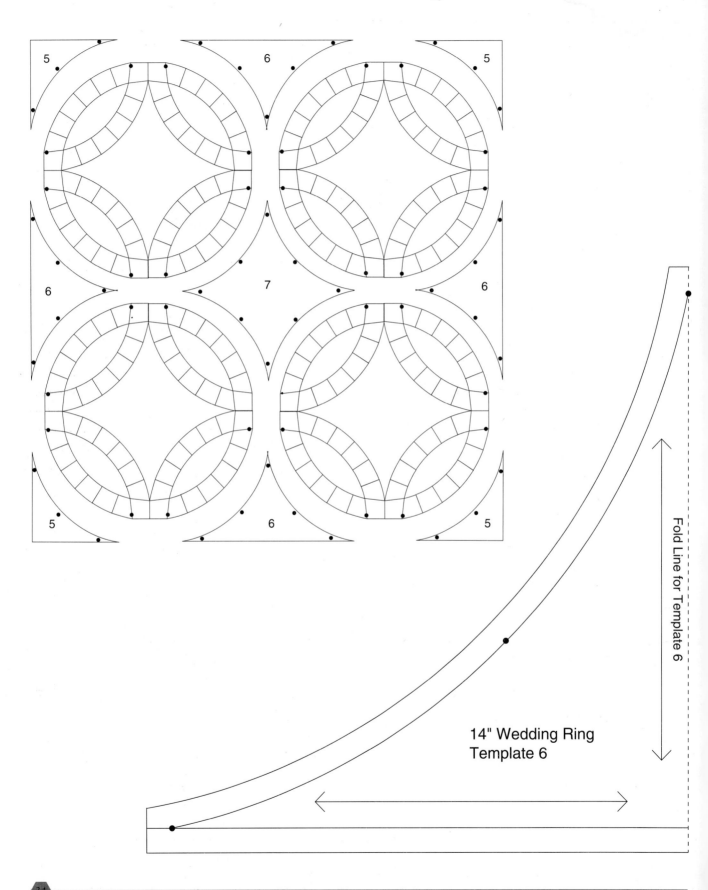

5   6   5

6   7   6

5   6   5

Fold Line for Template 6

14" Wedding Ring
Template 6

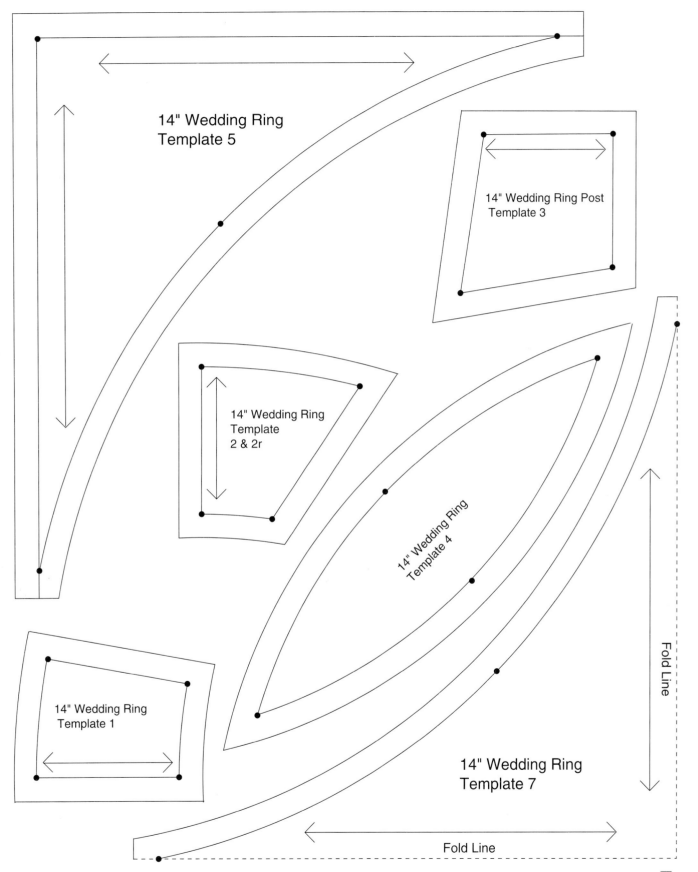

14" Wedding Ring
Template 5

14" Wedding Ring Post
Template 3

14" Wedding Ring
Template
2 & 2r

14" Wedding Ring
Template 4

14" Wedding Ring
Template 1

14" Wedding Ring
Template 7

Fold Line

Fold Line

SQUARE DANCE

A deceptively simple-looking quilt, made in light, medium and dark fabrics. The squares dancing across the surface are Puss in the Corner blocks set in counterpoint to each other. Wild Goose units create star shapes and the little Four Patch blocks cause the eye to travel over the surface.

QUILT SIZE 34 x 40 inches
BLOCK SIZE 4 inches
UNIT SIZE 1 inch

MATERIALS
(based on 42-inch fabric width)
Light fabric: 1½ yards
Medium fabric: 1½ yards
Dark fabric: 1½ yards
Backing fabric: 1¼ yards
2-oz polyester wadding: 1¼ yards

CUTTING
Inner border
From light fabric cut two strips 1½ x 30½ inches and two strips 26½ x 1½ inches.

Outer border
From medium fabric cut two strips 4½ x 32½ inches and two strips 4½ x 34½ inches.

Binding
From medium fabric cut four 2½-inch strips from selvedge to selvedge.

Blocks
Light fabric
1 Cut four 1½-inch strips from selvedge to selvedge. Slice into 100 1½-inch squares (Template 1).
2 Cut four 1½-inch strips. Slice into 38 rectangles 1½ x 2½ inches (Template 2).
3 Cut one 2½-inch strip. Slice into six 2½-inch squares (Template 3).
4 Cut one 2⅞-inch strip. Slice into nine 2⅞-inch squares. Cut each square in half diagonally to produce 18 half-square triangles (Template 4).
5 Cut four 2½-inch strips. Slice into 31 Wild Goose triangles (Template 5).

Medium fabric
1 Cut three 2⅞-inch strips. Slice into 40 2⅞-inch squares. Slice in half for 80 half-square triangles (Template 4).

Dark fabric
1 Cut four 1½-inch strips. Slice into 100 1½-inch squares (Template 1).
2 Cut three 1½-inch strips. Slice into 38 rectangles 1½ x 2½ inches (Template 2).
3 Cut one 2½-inch strip. Slice into six 2½-inch squares (Template 3).

Backing and wadding
From the backing fabric cut a rectangle 38 x 44 inches.

From the wadding cut a rectangle 38 x 44 inches.

CONSTRUCTION
Piecing the blocks
1 With medium and light triangles (Template 4) make 18 of unit A.

2 With dark and light 1½-inch squares (Template 1) make 24 of unit B.

3 With medium triangles and large light triangles (Templates 4 and 5) make 31 of unit C.

4 With light and dark small squares and rectangles (Templates 1 and 2) make 14 of unit D.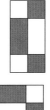

5 With dark rectangles and small and large light squares (Templates 1, 2 and 3) make six of unit E.

6 With light rectangles and small and large dark squares (Templates 1, 2 and 3) make six of unit F.

Piecing the rows
The units and completed blocks are now assembled into five different rows.

1 Make one Row A.

2 Make five of Row B.

3 Make two of Row C.

4 Make two of Row D.

5 Make one Row E.

Piecing the top

This is the tricky part. Make sure you have identified each row and placed it in the right direction. Lay out the rows in the sequence illustrated. Sew together.

Piecing the borders (illustration on facing page)

1 Attach the longer inner borders to either side of the quilt. Attach the remaining inner borders to the top and bottom.

2 Attach the shorter outer borders to either side of the quilt. Attach the remaining longer strips to the top and bottom.

QUILTING AND FINISHING

Press the quilt top, and tidy up any stray threads that may show through the fabric.

On a flat surface, smooth out the backing with the wrong side facing upwards. Secure with masking tape or with cloth clamps to prevent it from shifting. Unfold the wadding and pat it into place using a wooden rule to smooth it gently over the backing. Centre the quilt top right side up, over the wadding. Gently smooth out any ripples using the ruler and baste the sandwich together. See Skill Basics section, Basting the Sandwich for further details (page 56).

Quilt the sandwich. Bind the edge with continuous French binding (see page 58).

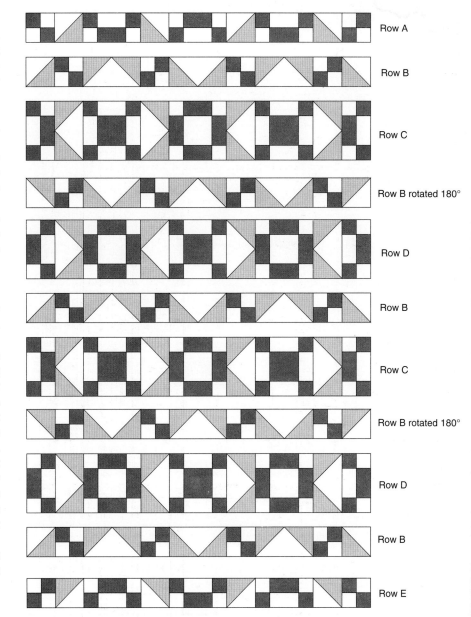

Row A

Row B

Row C

Row B rotated 180°

Row D

Row B

Row C

Row B rotated 180°

Row D

Row B

Row E

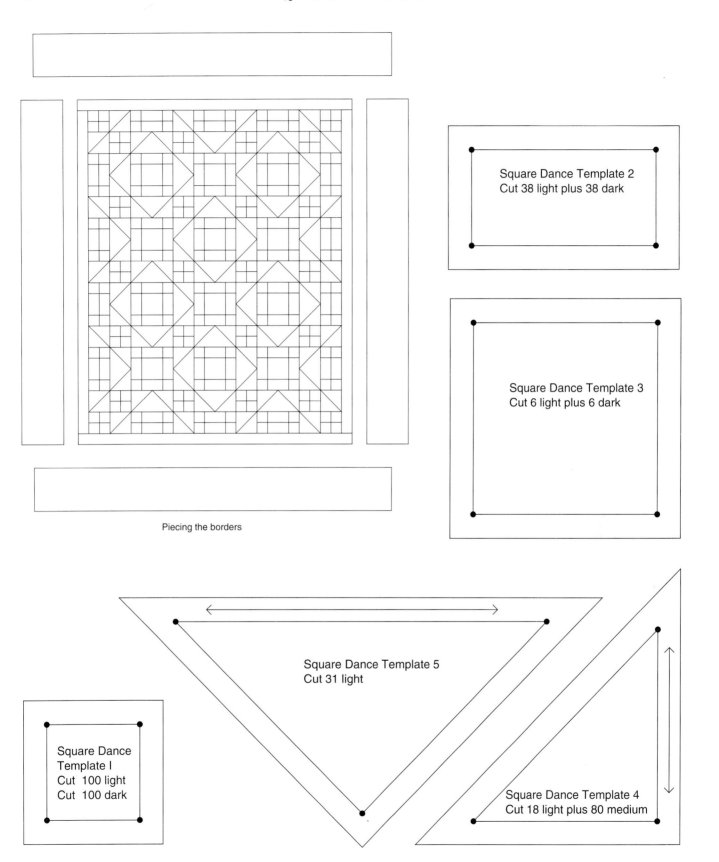

Piecing the borders

Square Dance Template 2
Cut 38 light plus 38 dark

Square Dance Template 3
Cut 6 light plus 6 dark

Square Dance Template 5
Cut 31 light

Square Dance
Template I
Cut 100 light
Cut 100 dark

Square Dance Template 4
Cut 18 light plus 80 medium

SOUTHALL POP

A salute to the Sixties and Pop Art. The small hanging of just five blocks in a diagonal set is made from handwoven Indian silk purchased from Southall in Middlesex. It looks simple but cutting, sewing and piecing the stripes will test the accuracy of your cutting and sewing (maintain an accurate ¼-inch seam allowance as you sew, as the slightest wobble will be visible).

QUILT SIZE	24 x 24 inches
STRIP SIZE	¾ inch

MATERIALS
(based on 42-inch fabric width)
Light fabric: ¼ yard
Dark fabric: ¾ yard
Backing fabric: 1 yard
2-oz polyester wadding: 1 yard

CUTTING
Border
From the dark fabric cut two strips of 3½ x 18½ inches and a further two strips of 3½ x 24½ inches.

Blocks
From the light fabric cut six 1¼-inch strips from selvedge to selvedge. From the dark fabric cut another six 1¼-inch strips.

Backing and wadding
Cut a square 28 x 28 inches from both the backing fabric and the wadding.

CONSTRUCTION
Piecing the blocks
1 Using a ¼-inch seam allowance, make two sets of strips, as shown below. Press the seams towards the darker material.

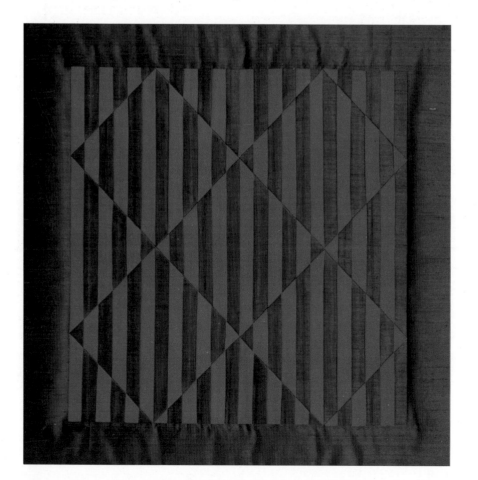

2 Refer to the cutting chart. The blocks are labelled to help with the piecing process. Two templates are required to cut the blocks. Be aware that some of the shapes are mirror images. It is important to cut the blocks exactly as shown, and to use a ¼-inch seam allowance.

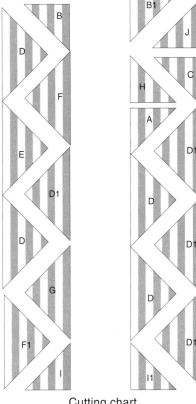

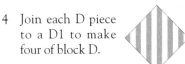

Cutting chart

3 Join pieces B and B1 to make one block B.

4 Join each D piece to a D1 to make four of block D.

5 Join pieces F and F1 to make one block F (a 180° rotation of block D).

6 Join pieces I and I1 to make one block I.

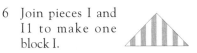

Piecing the top
1 Lay out the blocks as illustrated (right).
2 Piece the blocks together into the three diagonal rows. Sew Row 1 to Row 2. Then add Row 3. Finally add the corner triangles A and J to complete the piecing of the top.

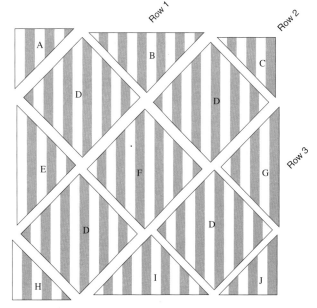

Borders
1 Attach the short borders to either side.
2 Add the longer borders to the top and bottom to complete the quilt top.

QUILTING AND FINISHING

Press the quilt top, and tidy up any stray threads that may show through the fabric.

On a flat surface, smooth out the backing with the wrong side facing upwards. Secure with masking tape or with cloth clamps to prevent it from shifting. Unfold the wadding and pat it into place using a wooden rule to smooth it gently over the backing. Centre the quilt top right side up, over the wadding. Gently smooth out any ripples using the ruler and baste the sandwich together. See Skill Basics section, Basting the Sandwich for further details (page 56).

Quilt the sandwich. The quilt in the photograph was laced on to a board and the back neatened by slip-stitching a lining piece around the edges. Velcro is used to fix the hanging.

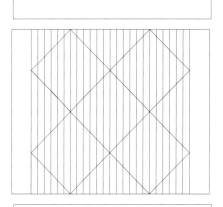

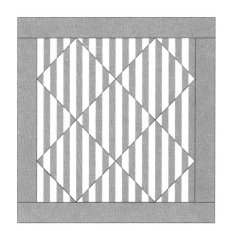

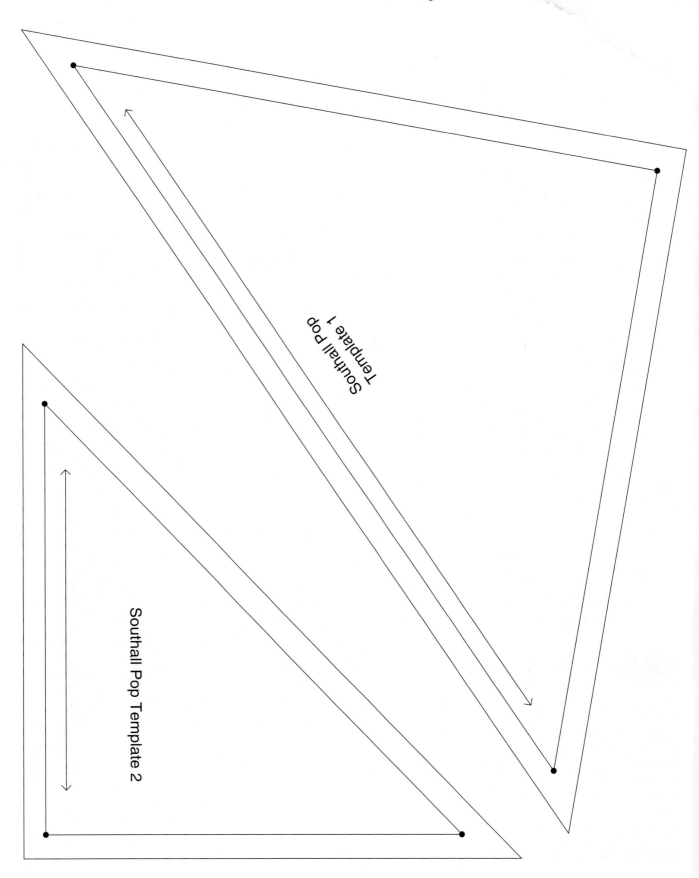

Southall Pop
Template 1

Southall Pop Template 2

OCEAN WAVE

The quilt is made of assorted blue scrap triangles set against a hand-dyed, pale blue background. It is constructed of irregular-shaped blocks set together in strips. A small, pieced Compass design provides a focus in the centre, and the surrounding squares have Fleurs de Lys appliquéd to their centres. There are two borders framing the quilt: a narrow accent strip surrounded by straight borders with corner squares. Full-size patterns for the templates are provided. They include paper guides which are used to speed up the half-square triangle construction process.

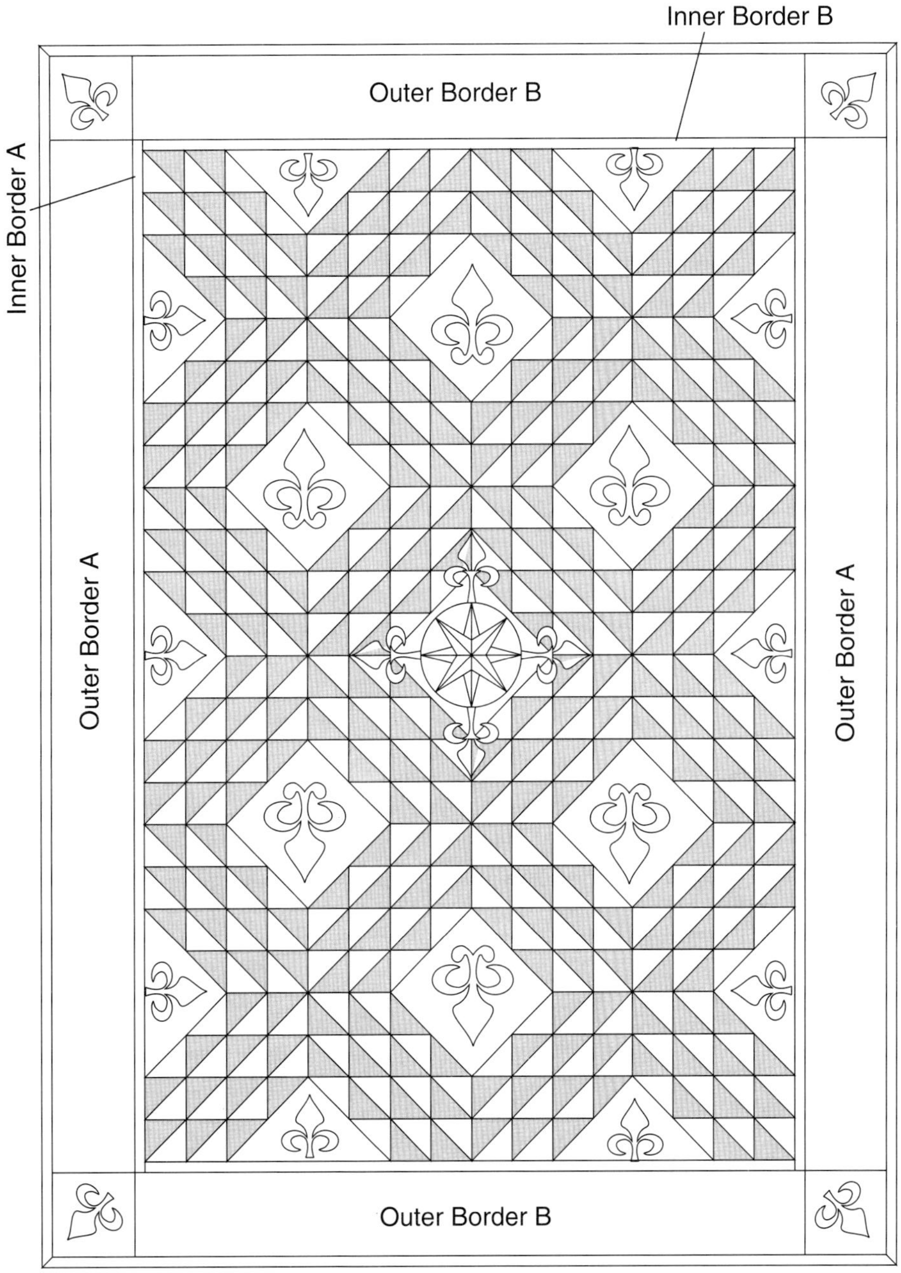

QUILT SIZE 41 x 58 inches

MAKING TEMPLATES

Appliqué templates: The three patterns required for the Fleur de Lys appliqué are given with no seam allowance. Make the templates and trace around the design onto the smooth side of the fusible web ready for fusing to the chosen fabric.

Ocean Wave and Compass templates: The patterns given include the seam allowance. Make the templates by tracing off the patterns given and sticking to template plastic or card. With an awl or a large tapestry needle, make a hole through the square and triangle templates exactly on the junction of the seam lines.

Inner Border B

Outer Border B

Inner Border A

Outer Border A

Outer Border A

Outer Border B

MATERIALS

Assorted scraps : 1½ yards
Paper-backed fusible web (such as Bondaweb): ¼ yard
Background colour: 2½ yards
Accent colour: 1½ yards
Contrast fabric: 1¾ yards
Backing fabric: 2 yards
2-oz polyester wadding: 2 yards

CUTTING

From the assorted scraps

1 Half-square triangle units: make sure the scrap fabrics are large enough to cut the 20 7 x 10-inch rectangles for speed piecing.
2 Loose triangles: using Ocean Wave Template 3, cut 48 triangles.
3 Half-square triangles: cut 20 rectangles 7 x 10 inches.
4 Compass templates (page 46): using Compass Template 1, cut eight background pieces from dark fabric. Mark the dots on the wrong side of the fabric. Using Compass Templates 2 and 3, mark and cut four pieces each from contrasting fabric. Mark the dots on the wrong side of the fabric.

From the fusible web

Using Fleur de Lys Templates 1, 2 and 3, mark four, fourteen and six shapes respectively onto the smooth side of the interlining.

From the background colour

Loose triangles: using Ocean Wave Template 3 cut 48 loose triangles.
Half-square triangle units: cut 20 rectangles 7 x 10½ inches (these will be cut into triangles later).
Plain squares: using Ocean Wave Template 1 cut seven squares.
Perimeter triangles: using Ocean Waves Template 2 cut ten triangles.

From the accent colour

Inner Border A: cut two strips 1 x 49½ inches
Inner Border B: cut two strips 1 x 32½ inches
Border squares: cut four squares 4½ x 4½ inches
Fleur de Lys: following manufacturer's instructions, fuse the bonding to the wrong side of the fabric. Cut out the Fleur de Lys shapes.

From the contrast fabric

Outer Border A: cut two strips 4½ x 49½ inches.
Outer Border B: cut two strips 4½ x 33½ inches.
Continuous binding: cut sufficient 2½-inch strips on the cross or weft grain to yield 6¼ yards of binding (see page 58).

From the backing fabric

Cut a rectangle 44 x 61 inches.

From the wadding

Cut a rectangle 44 x 61 inches.

CONSTRUCTION

Half-square triangle units

1 Make 20 copies of the fast triangle guide given on page 48. Cut around the paper guide on the line where scissors are indicated.
2 Place one background colour rectangle and one scrap rectangle right sides together. If necessary

pin to secure. Place the paper guide on top and secure with masking tape. With short stitch length, start sewing at the top corner. Following the direction of the arrows, sew along the dotted line. By pivoting at the corners it is possible to complete the sewing with one seam only. Cut along the solid lines, using rotary cutting equipment. Peel off the paper guide by folding down and tearing off the seam allowance portion first, gripping the seam firmly between finger and thumb. Press the seams to one side and trim the ears that appear at the corners of the squares.

Each 7 x 10½-inch rectangle will produce 12 half-square triangle units. Repeat the process until 240 units are completed.

Piecing the blocks

1 Using five half-square triangle units and two scrap triangles, make 12 A1 units.
2 Using five half-square triangle units and two background triangles make 12 A2 units.

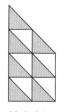 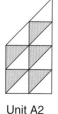

Unit A1   Unit A2

3 Make four A3 units using the dot-to-dot set-in seam construction method described in Skills Basics, page 53. Use one plain background square, two A1 units and two A2 units for each. (Refer

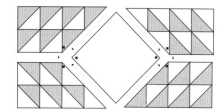

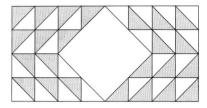

to the illustration at the bottom of the previous column for the piecing sequence.)

4 Make four A4 units, using one large plain background triangle, one A1 and one A2 unit for each.

5 Using five half-square triangle units and two small background triangles, make 12 B1 units.

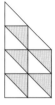   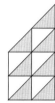

Unit B1   Unit B2

6 Using five half-square triangle units and two small scrap triangles make 12 B2 units.

7 Make six B3 units, each from one large plain background triangle, one B1 unit and one B2 unit.

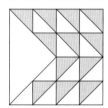

8 Make three B4 units, each using one plain background square, two B1s and two B2s.

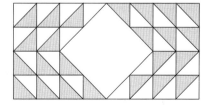

Piecing the compass

The compass on the quilt illustrated is made up of two fabrics: a dark blue background with a contrast colour for the compass points.

   Make sure that the templates are accurate. Pierce small holes at the seam junctions of the templates to allow dots to be transferred to the wrong side of the fabric.

1 Using the pin stabbing method (see Skill Basics, page 52) join together two pieces cut from Template 1 and one cut from Template 2 to make unit A: sew edge to edge along the seam line, right through the dot marks. Make four of unit A.

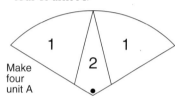

Make four unit A

2 Refer to the illustration below, and attach pieces cut from Template 3 to either side of unit A. Three separate seams are required to complete this unit.
(i) Pin stab through the dot marks to align the seam and sew the first seam AC from the outer edge,

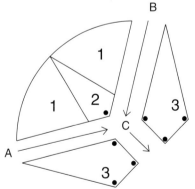

Make four unit B using set in seam construction method.

stopping the seam at the inner C dot marks – do not stitch into the seam allowance!
(ii) Pin stab through the dots to align the seam and sew the second

seam BC from the outer edge B, stopping the seam at the inner C dot marks – again, do not stitch into the seam allowance!
(iii) Pin stab through the dots to align the seam. Sew the third seam CD from the three dots at point C to the outer edge of the unit.

3 Refer to the illustration below for the five-seam sequence required to complete the compass circle.

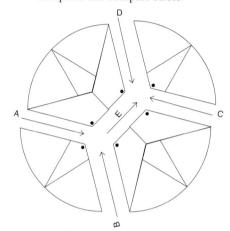

Piecing sequence to complete compass star.

4 Carefully press the completed circle. Fold under the seam allowance. Baste around the edge of the compass. Slip stitch to the centre of a background square on unit B4. Refer to the main illustration on page 43.

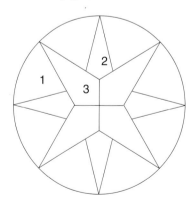

Fleur de Lys appliqué

1 Fuse the four small number 1 Fleur de Lys shapes to the four points of the compass design. Secure the edges with a zig-zag or satin stitch.

2 Fuse ten number 2 Fleur de Lys shapes to the perimeter triangles and secure the edges with a zig-zag or satin stitch. Fuse the remaining remaining four shapes to the accent coloured border squares in the same way.

3 Fuse the six large number 3 Fleur de Lys shapes to the background squares and secure the edges with a zig-zag or satin stitch.

Quilt top construction sequence
The illustration in the centre of this page shows the construction sequence for the quilt top. Piece the units together into seven rows and then join the rows one to another to complete the panel.

Attaching the borders
1 Sew Inner Border A strips to either side of the quilt top.
2 Sew Inner Border B strips to top and bottom.
3 Sew Outer Border A strips to either side.

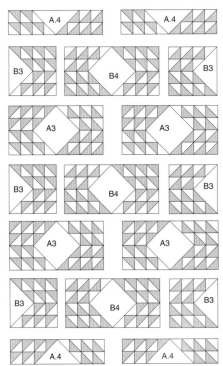

4 Sew a border square to either end of each Border B strip and attach to the top and bottom of the quilt.

For more detailed instructions see Skill Basics section (page 55).

QUILTING AND FINISHING
Press the quilt top, and tidy up any stray threads that may show through the fabric. Press the backing fabric.

On a flat surface, smooth out the backing with the wrong side facing upwards. Secure with masking tape or with cloth clamps to prevent it from shifting. Unfold the wadding and pat it into place using a wooden rule to smooth it gently over thebacking. Centre the quilt top right side up, over the wadding. Gently smooth out any ripples using the ruler and baste the sandwich together. See Skill Basics section, Basting the Sandwich for further details.

Quilt around the triangle shapes with quilting lines extending out into the edge of the border area. Outline quilting around the appliqué and compass shapes will add extra loft and texture to the quilt (see page 56).

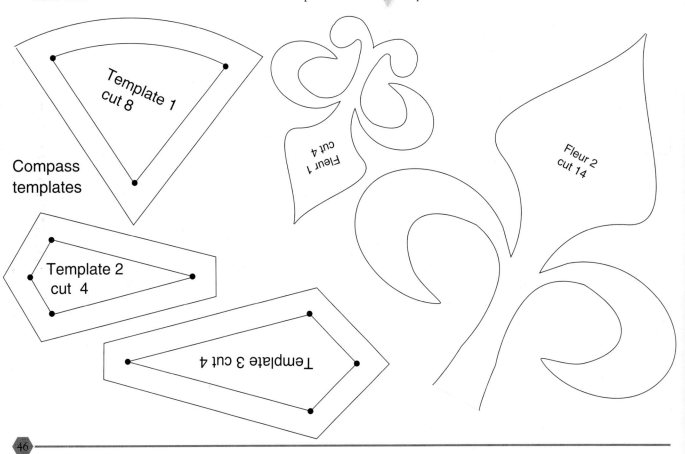

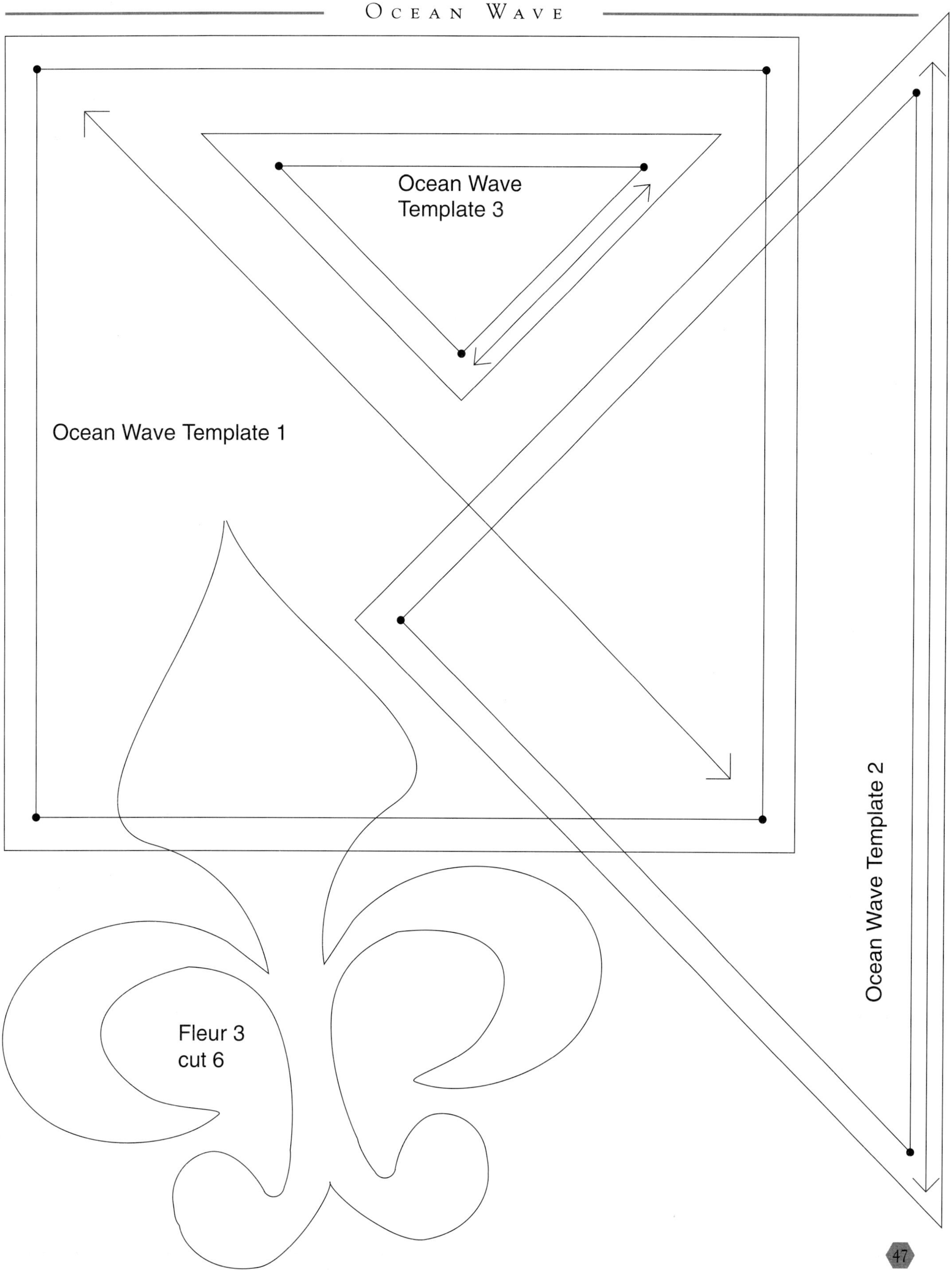

Ocean Wave
Template 3

Ocean Wave Template 1

Ocean Wave Template 2

Fleur 3
cut 6

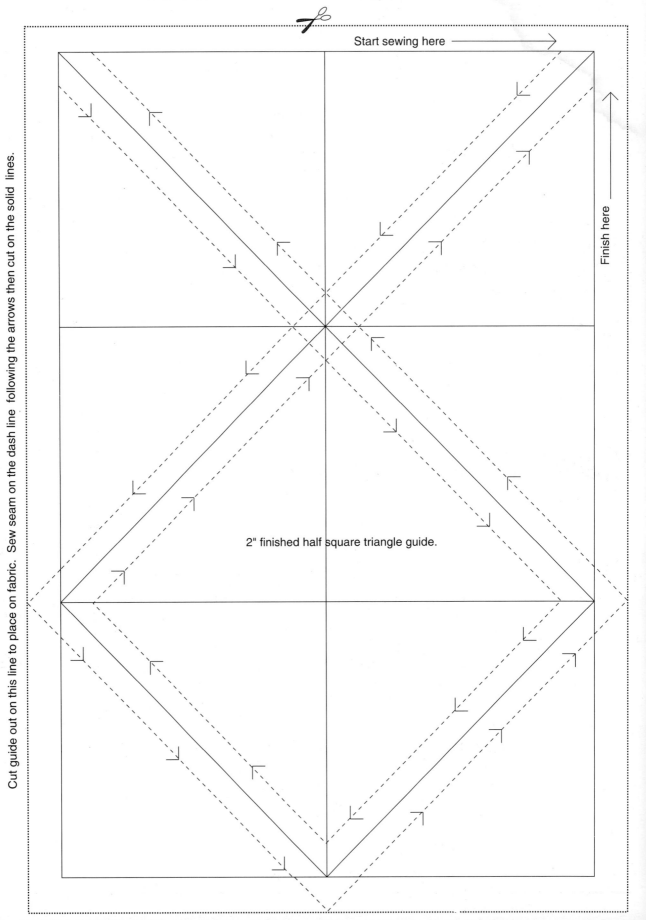

Start sewing here →

Finish here →

Cut guide out on this line to place on fabric. Sew seam on the dash line following the arrows then cut on the solid lines.

2" finished half square triangle guide.

Skill Basics

Contents

This section provides full details of techniques used in the projects in this book.
Experienced patchworkers will find it useful when working on their own designs.

SEWING KIT

A basic sewing kit for patchwork includes:

Needles Betweens are the traditional quilting needles. Number 8 is a good size to start with. The higher the number, the smaller and finer the needle. Straws are used for basting and Sharps for general piecing and appliqué work.

Thimbles Use one that fits well and has a raised edge around the rim.

Pins Sharp, shiny slender dressmakers' pins. Specialist, slender flower-headed pins are a luxury well worth having. Put them on your family wish-list if you feel they are an extravagance.

Scissors Sharp fabric scissors, embroidery scissors, thread snips.

Toning thread Ecru is a good staple colour as are shades of grey and brown.

A good-sized seam ripper – not just for unpicking seams but also helpful for guiding the patches through the sewing machine.

CUTTING EQUIPMENT

The rotary cutter has revolutionised the whole patchwork process and comes in two sizes. The larger one is best for patchwork. They have extremely sharp circular blades and should be handled with care. Some have straight handles, others have curved handles, and some are equipped with spring-loaded safety guards. Keep all cutters in a safe place, well away from tiny fingers.

Whatever type you buy, always roll the cutter away from you and be sure to replace the safety guard every time a cut is finished.

Rotary ruler These rulers are made of thick transparent plastic and are used to guide the rotary cutter. They come in a bewildering variety of types. The best to buy are the 6 x 24-inch Omnigrid rulers. They have both yellow and black markings making a horizontal and vertical grid at ⅛-inch intervals. They are also marked with 30°, 45° and 60°. The grid and the angles enable the ruler to be used both as a T-square and as a right angle.

Some patchworkers have a collection of rotary rulers – the Trudy Hughes Rotary Mate is a very useful size for cutting smaller pieces.

Cutting mat The mat is essential to protect both the table top and the blade of the rotary cutter. A useful size is 24 x 18 inches. Make sure that the mat you buy has a grid marked on it which is helpful when straightening the fabric. Some mats are marked with 45° lines, which are useful when cutting bias strips.

Fabric-cutting scissors If you are not yet ready to make the investment in rotary cutting equipment make sure that your fabric shears are well sharpened. Never allow fabric-cutting scissors to be used for cutting paper or template-making material.

Embroidery scissors A small pair of scissors is useful for trimming seams and for appliqué work. Test the scissors to make sure that the blades will cut right up to the tips.

Paper-cutting scissors Keep a pair of scissors for cutting paper, card and template plastic.

SEWING MACHINE

Buy the best you can afford. Just remember it is not necessary to buy a top-of-the-range computerised model. The minimum features to look for are:

- **First-class easily adjustable tension**
- **Easily adjustable stitch length**
- **A good even straight stitch**
- **A good satin stitch**
- **An invisible hem stitch.**

Highly desirable features include:

- **A feed dog that will disengage to allow free-motion sewing**
- **A variable needle stop position (either up or down)**
- **A two-speed motor**
- **A walking foot**
- **A ¼-inch foot.**

Avoid machines where the tension and the stitch length are not easily adjustable. Take along the kind of fabric you will use to have a test run on a possible purchase. If the dealer is not happy for you to try the machine then do not buy it.

Read your manual, clean and de-fluff the machine regularly, change needles frequently, have it serviced by a reputable dealer.

FABRIC SELECTION

Choose 100% cottons for ease of use. Avoid polycottons, they are stubborn, unforgiving and difficult to sew. Silks look stunning in patchwork. The most suitable is Honan silk which is quite stable and does not fray as easily as other varieties. If recycling materials, choose the best parts and ruthlessly discard worn, frayed or thinning bits.

FABRIC PREPARATION

Whether you decide to pre-wash fabric is a personal decision. It is wise to test for colour fastness especially for dark red and blue colours, which are notoriously fugitive dyes. To stabilise soft, floppy fabrics, use spray starch to give a good crisp finish which will greatly aid precision in marking and piecing. If the starch is not sufficient, try using the lightest-weight iron-on interfacing to give some body.

FABRIC MARKING
Different types of fabric will require different types of marker, depending on the colour and pattern. The most useful are: HB pencils, silver pencils, chalk markers, water-soluble blue pens, waterproof ink pens, and when all else fails a fineline ballpoint. Always test your chosen marker to be certain it will meet your requirements.

Lay the template **face down** on the **wrong** side of the fabric making sure that the straight grain aligns with the grainline marking on the template. Trace around the template shape as accurately as possible, and make dot marks at the seam junctions where appropriate.

MAKING TEMPLATES
Templates are best made from easily-cut vinyl or plastic sheets. They can be made from manilla card or cardboard, but these are not so durable.
1 Secure a piece of tracing paper over the pattern with some low-tack masking tape. Carefully trace the pattern shape. These traced lines are the **seam lines**. Mark a dot at each corner.
2 Use a ruler to draft the ¼-inch allowance all the way round the shape. This second line is the the **cutting line**. Carefully peel away the masking tape and remove the tracing paper.
3 Glue the tracing paper to the template material (if plastic, check the glue is suitable).

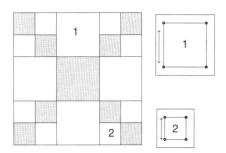

4 Carefully cut out the template on the **outer** (cutting) line. Using an awl (and a piece of waste wood to protect the table top) pierce a hole through the dots marked at each seam junction. Smooth the back of the holes with fine sandpaper and test that it is possible to mark a dot onto fabric, through the hole in the template (see illustration).
5 Label each template with its number, block name, and direction of grain.

ROTARY CUTTING
Generally, when using the rotary cutter, the fabric is cut in strips from selvedge edge to selvedge edge (on the cross or weft grain). First it is important to straighten the edge of the fabric so the strips will be cut straight and at right angles to the selvedge edges. Guidelines are given for a right-handed method.

Straightening the edge of the fabric
1 Fold the fabric selvedge to selvedge and press the fold. Fold in half again by aligning the fold against the selvedge edges, making four layers of fabric. Press the new fold.
2 Line up the folded edge of the fabric with a line on the cutting board with the bulk of the fabric to your left (see illustration).

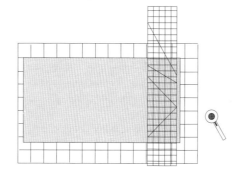

3 Place the ruler at right angles to the selvedge and align it with the markings on the edges of the cutting mat.
4 Place your left hand on the ruler, press down firmly holding the cutter in your right hand. Slide the cutter along the bottom of the board from right to left until it hits the ruler.
5 Release the safety catch and take a

smooth firm cut away from yourself, keeping the blade of the cutter tight against the edge of the ruler. Return the safety guard as soon as the cut is made.
6 Turn the mat around so that the bulk of the fabric is now on you right hand side and you are ready to start cutting strips the width you require (see illustration).

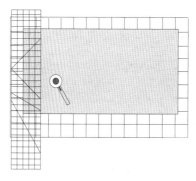

HAND SEWING
Piecing the blocks
Analyse the block to see how it can best be sewn. Sew the smallest patches into small units first. Then join the units into rows, and finally join the rows to complete the block.

Hand piecing
After the fabric pieces have been cut and marked lay them out in the sequence they will be pieced. Use neutral-coloured threads. Beige or ecru and mid greys are good staple colours. When sewing a dark patch to a light one match the thread to the fabric towards which you will be pressing the seam allowance. Generally sew the tiny pieces into small units first. Then sew the units into rows, and finally join the rows to complete the block.

The simple seam
The hand-pieced simple seam is a

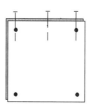

straight seam joining two patches together. It runs from dot to dot along the seam line. To join two patches place them right sides together. Pin them together exactly on the marked dots, placing the pins at right angles to the sewing line. Start the seam line at the dot and take one or two back stitches to secure. Sew with a small running stitch right through the dot, and take another backstitch every two or three stitches. Remove any pins as you go, finishing the seam with a couple of back stitches at the dot marking the end of the seam. Press towards the darker fabric.

The seam joint

A seam joint occurs where two or more seams cross or converge. For example in the four patch, four seams meet at the centre of the block. Align and pin two units of joined squares together and pin at the dots. Place a further

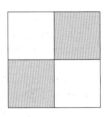

pin the centre of the seam, exactly at the point where the opposing seams butt up against each other. Begin the seam at the dot mark with a couple of short backstitches and sew with short running stitches to the pin at the butted seam. Hold the seam allowance out of the way and take a small back-

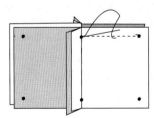

stitch. Do not sew across the seam allowance, just slip the needle through

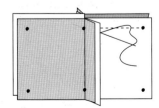

the seam. Flip the seam allowances towards the seam just sewn and continue sewing. End the seam at the dot mark with a couple of back-stitches. Machine-sewn seams are sewn from edge to edge.

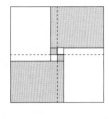

Machine Piecing

Accurate cutting is required for machine piecing, which is why templates for machine piecing always include the seam allowances. The rotary cutter is a great aid in precision, and it is essential that the ¼-inch seam allowance on your sewing machine exactly matches the ¼-inch seam allowance used when cutting the fabric.

Quarter-inch seam allowance

If the presser foot on your machine is ¼ inch wide, align the cut edge of the fabric with the edge of the presser foot. Seams are generally sewn from edge to edge of the fabric. Set in seams are an exception to this rule.

If a ¼-inch presser foot is not available it is help-ful to mark the ¼-inch allow-ance on your machine with a piece of masking tape to guide the edge of the fabric (see illustration).

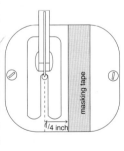

Chain piecing simple seams

Organise the patches in the sequence they are to be pieced and wherever possible chain piece to save time and thread. Place the patches right sides together and sew a seam from edge to edge. Do not remove

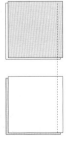

the patches from the sewing machine. Place the next pair of patches under the presser foot and sew as seam from edge to edge. Continue this sequence until all the patches are sewn. As the process is continued a long line of patches like a miniature line of bunting is produced. Use thread snip-pers to snip the thread between each unit.

Types of Seam

Joints and points; pin stabbing

Joints and points occur where two or more seam lines converge. The extra bulk of the fabric meeting the feed dogs of the machine makes pin stab-bing a must for precision seam match-ing. The illustration below shows pin

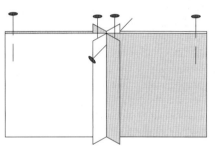

stabbing at the seam joint on a four-patch unit. Stab the pin right through the seam line of the matching patches and pull it through tightly. Hold the patches together firmly, peel back the seam allowances to confirm that the seam lines are still perfectly aligned and secure a further two pins, one on each side of the stabbed pin and as close as possible to it. Remove the stab pin and sew a perfectly matching seam.

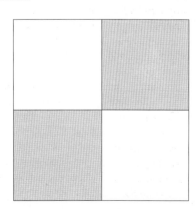

Where a pointed angled seam hits a seam line as in this illustration, aim

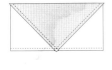

the needle of the machine to pass directly through the middle of the X junction formed by the stitching lines.

Set in seams

A set in seam occurs where two patches form an angle into which a third patch is inserted.

They are sometimes referred to as 'Y' seams. With a little preparation and some accurate sewing they are not difficult to piece. Make sure that the patches to be pieced are accurately cut and have dots marked on the seam junction points as illustrated below.

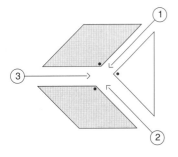

The example given shows the sequence of sewing when setting in a triangle to two diamond patches.

1 *Refer to the illustration (next column) and with the triangle on top of the diamond patch sew the first seam from the edge of the fabric to the dot mark. Backstitch at this point and do not sew into the seam allowance.*

2 *Turn the unit and place the second diamond patch underneath the triangle and sew the second seam from the edge of the fabric up to the dot mark. Backstitch at this point and do not sew into the seam allowance.*

3 *Align the edges of the diamonds and sew the final seam from the edge of the fabric up to the dot mark and backstitch to finish the set in seam.*

Curved seams

Machine piecing curves is not so difficult but does require accurate templates with balance marks along the curves. The example gives the stages in marking, cutting and sewing a Drunkards Path patch.

1 *Place the two templates required, face down on the wrong side of the fabric with the straight edge on the straight grain. Cut out the fabric shapes accurately along the marked lines and clearly mark the balance points.*

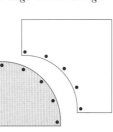

2 *With right sides together place the small convex patch on top of the*

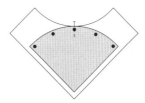

concave piece. Pin through the centre balance marks, weaving the pin in and out twice to secure it.

3 *Pin either end of the curve through the balance marks, aligning the straight edges before pinning.*

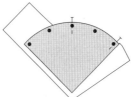

Pin each end of the curve

4 *Pin twice more, carefully matching the balance marks, easing the piece as you secure the patches.*

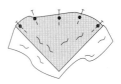

5 *Sew with a ¼-inch seam allowance, Press the seam allowance towards the concave curve.*

Half way seams

Half way seams are partially sewn seams that avoid the necessity of setting in a seam. They occur in blocks like the one illustrated.

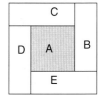

1 *Begin with the centre square A. Align strip B with the bottom of the square and sew a seam half way along the side of the*

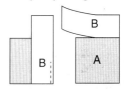

square and back tack. Rotate the unit 90° to the left (anticlockwise).

2 *Place strip C on top of the square and sew the seam from edge to edge. Rotate the unit 90° to the left.*

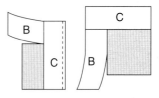

3 *Place strip D on top of the square and sew the seam from edge to edge as*

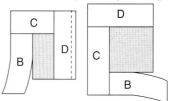

illustrated. Turn the unit 90° to the left.

4   *Repeat the process with strip E.*

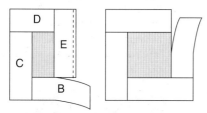

5   *Complete the seam along the edge of strip B to complete the partial seam unit.*

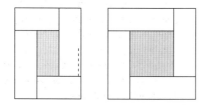

Pressing

The aim is to have the fabric surface as smooth as possible. The nature of the fabric and type of construction method used will dictate what strategy to use for pressing seams. In general terms it is advisable to press the seam allowances to one side where hand piecing has been used. If you use the sewing machine you will probably discover that a combination of pressing seams open and pressing to one side will work for you .

Setting the Blocks Together

There are many ways of setting the blocks together – here are two of the most popular.

Straight sets
Blocks are set side by side in rows.

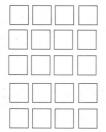

1   *Lay the blocks out on a flat surface to check positioning.*

2   *Sew together each row of blocks as illustrated, pin stabbing and basting to match joints and points perfectly.*

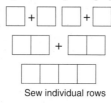

Sew individual rows

4   *Sew the rows together into sections.*

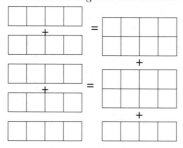

Sew rows into sections

5   *Join the sections to complete the top.*

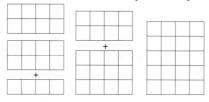

Diagonal sets
Blocks are turned on point and set together diagonally. Setting and corner triangles are used around the edges to complete the rectangular shape.

1   *Lay the blocks out on a flat surface to check positioning.*

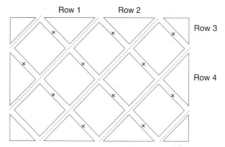

2   *Sew one row at a time as illustrated. It is wise to replace the blocks to their places in the row each time a seam is sewn.*

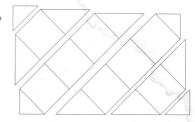

3   *Lay out all the sewn rows in sequence and sew each row together. Check the position of the sequence after each seam has been sewn and finally attach the remaining corner triangles to complete the piecing of the top.*

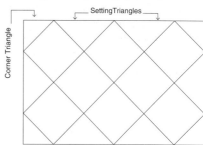

Borders

Measuring and cutting borders
To enable the quilt to hang square the borders should be cut the same length as measurements taken through the centre of the top. Because of the tendency of the edges of a pieced top to stretch it is important not to use the edge measurements. Directions are given for fitting the three most popular types of border.

Straight borders

1   *Borders are cut to the finished width plus seam allowances. To determine the length to be cut, measure length A through the centre. To this measurement add 2 inches for a working allowance and cut two borders this length.*

2 Mark the centre of the long edges by folding the quilt in half (so the top and bottom edges meet), then pin-mark

the centre point of the edge. Fold a border strip in half and mark its centre with a securely fastened pin. Measure in each direction from the centre of the border strip half the measurement determined in step 1. Weave a pin in and out to mark each spot. Repeat the process with the second long border strip.

3 Lay one of the border strips on top of the long edge of the quilt matching the pins to the centre and the corner edge

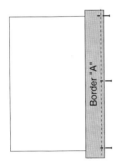

of the quilt top. Pin baste along the edges – it may be necessary to ease the quilt top to fit the borders.

4 Use a rotary ruler or right angle to square the borders with the quilt top as illustrated and trim the excess fabric with a rotary cutter.

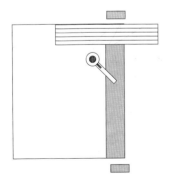

5 Measure length B across the centre (including the attached border strips) and add 2 inches as a working allowance.

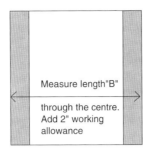

Measure length "B" through the centre. Add 2" working allowance

6 Cut two borders this length and repeat steps 2–4 to complete the border.

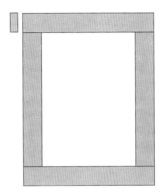

Borders with corner squares

1 Borders are cut the finished width plus seam allowances. To determine the length to be cut, measure length A

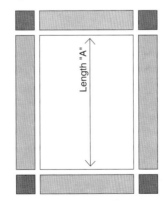

through the centre. To this measurement add 2 inches for a working allowance and cut two borders this length. The width will be the finished width of the border plus ½ inch for the seam allowances.

2 Mark the centre of the long edges by folding the quilt in half (so the top and bottom edges meet), then pin-mark the centre point of the edge. Fold a

border strip in half and mark its centre with a securely fastened pin. Measure in each direction from the centre of the border strip half the measurement determined in step 1. Weave a pin in and out to mark the spot. Repeat the process with the second border strip.

3 Lay one of the border strips on top of the edge of the quilt matching the pins to the centre and corner edge of the quilt top. Pin-baste along the edges, easing the quilt top where necessary to fit the borders.

4 Use a rotary ruler or right angle to square the borders with the quilt top and trim the excess fabric.

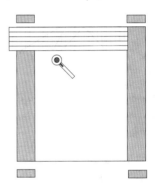

5 Measure length B through the centre of the quilt. Cut two border strips to this dimension plus ½ inch for the seam allowances. Attach corner squares to either end of each strip.

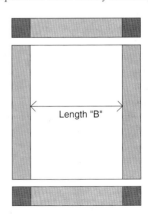

6 *Lay a border strip on top of the quilt top and pin baste, matching the seam allowances and easing the quilt top where necessary. Repeat with the final border strip to complete the quilt top.*

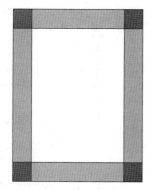

Mitred borders

These always look good with diagonal sets and with striped border fabric. They are cut the length of the quilt, plus twice the finished width of the border, plus 4 inches working allowance. The width to cut is the finished width, plus seam allowances.

1 *Press the quilt top and make a dot mark ¼ inch in from each of the four corners. See illustration and measure length A through the centre of the quilt. Mark the centre of the long edges by folding the quilt in half* (so the top and bottom edges meet), then pin-mark the centre of the edge.

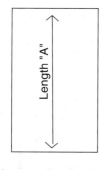

2 *Fold one of the long border strips in half and pin to mark the centre. Measure in each direction from the centre, and pin mark half the measurement determined in step 1.*

3 *Mark a dot on the seam line ¼ inch in from the marker pins to indicate the start and finish of the seam line.*

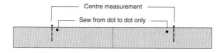

Fold, pin and mark the second border strip in the same way.

4 *Measure across the centre of the quilt to establish dimension B.*

5 *Fold one of the remaining border strips in half and pin to mark the centre. Measure out in each direction from the centre, half the measurement determined in step 4 and pin mark. Mark the seam dots on each strip as in step 3. Fold, pin and mark the remaining border strip in the same way.*

6 *Starting at the centre pins and with a border strip on top, pin baste the border strip to the quilt top. Match the pins to the centre of the top and pin stab the seam dots to secure the border. Complete the pin basting, easing the quilt top where required to the border strip. Start and stop the seam on the marked dots. Do not sew into the seam allowance at the corner*

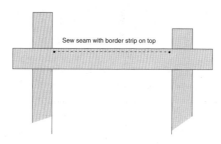

points. Begin and end each seam with a back tack. Repeat this process until all the borders are attached to the top.

Marking the mitre

For this next step you will require a rotary ruler that has a 45° angle marked on it (as illustrated).

1 *Press the seams and the entire top. Smooth out the top wrong side up on a flat surface. Starting at one of the bottom corners, adjust the border strips so that the side border strip folds back diagonally on itself, lying parallel to the bottom strip. Pin if necessary to secure, then press.*

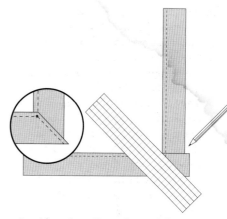

2 *Align the 45° marking of the ruler on the quilt top, with the edge of the ruler crossing through the seam dot as illustrated. Mark a diagonal line on the border strip to indicate the seam line.*

3 *Baste the seam from the inner dot to the outer edge of the quilt. Check from the front to ensure the corner is hanging straight and make any fine adjustments necessary before pressing the seam and sewing on the creased line to complete the corner.*

QUILTING
Basting the sandwich

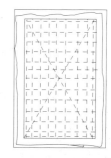

The quilt sandwich consists of the completed top, the wadding and a backing fabric. Many kinds of wadding are available: 2-oz polyester wadding is suitable for a beginner. Like the backing, wadding should be cut 2 inches larger all round than the quilt top. The backing fabric should be of similar weight to and in harmony with the quilt top. Avoid having a seam running down the centre of the lining.

Use a scratchproof table top to lay out the sandwich. The quilt is basted to prevent the layers from shifting during the quilting process. Use white basting thread to avoid coloured fibres becoming trapped in the surface of the quilt and in the wadding.

1   Use masking tape to mark the centre of the table top and also mark the centre point of each of the sides.
2   Thoroughly press the quilt top and tidy any stray thread that may show through (the last thing you want is have dark wisps of thread trapped and visible in the sandwich when you have finished quilting and binding the quilt).
3   The quilting design may be marked either before or after the sandwich is basted. A complicated feather design is likely to be marked prior to basting, unless stencils are used to mark it from the top.
4   Fold the backing fabric in two with wrong sides together. Fold in two again. Mark the centre point with a loose tacking thread that is easily removable. Also mark the centre point of each edge with a sharp crease.
5   Place the centre point of the backing on to the marked centre of the table and carefully unfold the fabric, making sure that it lies square on the table, aligning the halfway creases with the masking tape. Clamp in place with cloth clamps or with bull-dog clips (the ones with long arms that fold back on themselves).
6   Fold the wadding into four and thread mark the centre in the same way as the backing. Put the centre fold on the marked centre of the backing and gently unfold the wadding smoothing it out with a yardstick. Be careful not to stretch the wadding at all. Undo the clamps and reclamp the two layers together.
7   Fold the quilt top in two, right sides together and then fold again and lightly crease the centre of the sides. Match the centre to the centre of the wadding. Gently unfold the quilt top over the wadding, being careful to keep it square. Use a wooden yard rule to gently smooth out any bumps. Unclamp and then reclamp the three layers together.

8   From the centre out baste diagonal rows of basting stitches towards each corner of the table. Use a dessert spoon to help with the basting process, by placing it firmly on the quilt sandwich, just in front of where you wish the needle to emerge. Make the basting stitches around 1 inch long.
9   Continue the basting in straight lines horizontally and vertically creating a grid of rows about 3–4 inches apart. As each area is completed, unclamp and slide it across the table top ready for the next area to be basted Starting with the backing fabric smooth the layers over the table top, one by one. Reclamp and continue this process until the basting is complete.
10 Finish off with a row of small basting stitches right around the edges of the quilt.

Hand quilting
The purpose of the quilting stitch is to firmly lock the layers of the quilt together. A simple running stitch is generally used. Sometimes the stitches are extremely small, and sometimes they are extremely large. Although small stitches are favoured by 'experts' the size of the stitch is not so crucial. The important thing is to aim to make the stitches as even and as regular as possible. It helps to wear a thimble on the middle finger of the sewing hand and one on the forefinger of the other hand to stop the needle pricking your finger.

Quilting needles
Betweens are the traditional choice of hand quilters. A number eight is a suitable size for beginners. The higher the number the finer and shorter the needle. A short needle helps to keep the stitches small and evenly spaced.

Quilting thread
Specialised thread is available in a good range of colours. 100% cotton thread is the favourite, although poly-cotton threads are often used. Cut short lengths of around 18 inches to sew with. Knot the cut end of the

thread, and pull the thread through the fabric in the same direction that the needle is travelling to avoid excess friction creating tangled threads.

Quilting designs
There are many sources for quilt designs. Often pieced blocks are outline quilted about ¼ inch around the patches. The illustrations given show outline quilting for some blocks, together with some traditional filler and border designs.

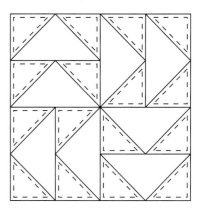

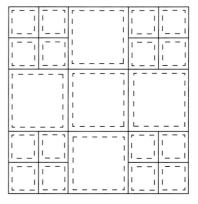

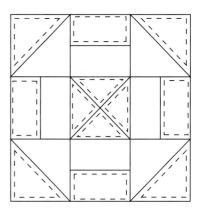

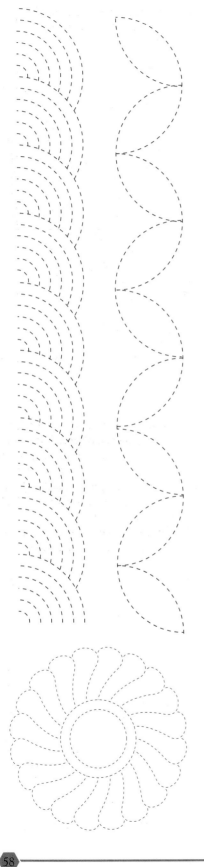

FINISHING

Hanging sleeve

The time to fix a hanging sleeve to a quilt is when the quilting is completed, the excess wadding and backing have been trimmed, and before the binding is applied. The depth of the sleeve will be determined by the depth of the batten you use to display the quilt.

1 Determine the width of the quilt top, and plan to have the sleeve to finish around two or three inches narrower than this dimension.

2 Cut a strip of cloth 6 inches wide by the required length. Fold in half, right sides together along the long edge and, using a ½-inch seam allowance, sew two seams along each short edge.

3 Turn right sides out, align the raw edges and press the seams and along the entire length of the sleeve. Fold in half lengthwise and finger press to mark the centre point.

4 Match the centre point of the raw edged side of the sleeve to the centre point of the quilt edge and pin baste along the top. Sew a scant ¼-inch seam along the edge to secure. Pin baste the lower edge of the sleeve and slip stitch to the quilt, making sure the stitches do not go through to the front of the quilt.

Continuous French binding

This is a strong and durable binding. It can be made from both straight cut and bias cut strips. Straight strips should be cut from selvedge to selvedge along the weft grain. The weft has greater elasticity than the warp or long grain and helps to give the binding a smooth, tailored look.

1 Cut sufficient 2½-inch strips, selvedge to selvedge to go around the perimeter of the quilt, plus an extra 14 inches.

2 The strips are joined by cutting the ends of each strip at 45° with a rotary

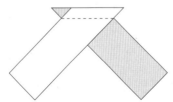

ruler and joining one to the other at right angles along the bias edge. You will notice that as the strips are placed at right angles to each other a triangle appears at either edge. The seam should run exactly between the spots where the triangles emerge from the long edges of the strips.

3 Mark a line parallel to, and 1 inch away from the bias edge on the wrong side of the fabric.

4 Fold the long edges of the binding wrong sides together along the long edge and press with a hot iron to make a sharp crease along the folded edge.

5 Align the raw edges of the binding strip on the right side of the quilt edge. Start with the marked end of the binding strips, half way down one of the long sides. Leave a spare 6–7 inch tail of binding before starting to sew the binding to the quilt top. Start with a few back stitches to secure the seam and use a generous ¼-inch seam allowance.

6 Stop sewing exactly ¼ inch from the corner of the quilt and sink the needle at this spot. Lift the presser foot. Pivot the quilt 90°. Let down the presser foot and reverse stitch in a straight line off the edge of the quilt.

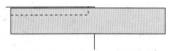

Cut the thread.

7 Fold the binding strip back on itself, 90° away from the horizontal edge of the quilt making a diagonal fold at the corner. Use a seam ripper or similar tool to hold the fold securely and fold the binding back down towards you so that the raw edges are now parallel with the vertical edge of the quilt. Use the

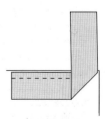

seam ripper to ease the fold so that it extends very slightly beyond the edge just sewn.

8   Sink the needle and sew from the horizontal edge until you reach the point ¼ inch away from the next corner where steps 6 and 7 are repeated. Continue the process until all four corners are complete.

9   Carry on sewing around the final corner and stop the seam at approximately 12 inches distance from the original starting point. Take a couple of back stitches to secure. Cut the binding leaving a tail of around 7 inches.

10   Take the binding strip with the pencil mark 1 inch from the edge and smooth it along the edge of the quilt. Lay the second binding tail on top of the marked strip. At the pencil mark fold the top strip back on itself along the marked line, opening out each strip. Finger press and cut the second strip on the fold line. Align the two

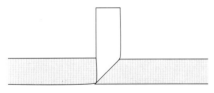

edges at 90° to each other and with small stitches tack a ½-inch seam. Refold the joined strips on the long edge and test to ensure that the binding lies flatly on the quilt surface. Make any adjustments necessary. Machine sew the short joining seam

and then complete the seam sewing the binding to the quilt.

11   Turn the binding to the back of the quilt and slipstitch along the folded edge taking care that the stitches do not penetrate the surface of the quilt top. At each corner fold the fabric to make tiny mitred corners which you

may or may not slipstitch as you please.

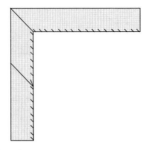

Bias binding

Bias binding is applied to a quilt edge using exactly the same construction methods as above. The only difference is that the 2½-inch wide fabric strips are cut on the bias. Bias binding uses lots of fabric and if used on a straight edge often gives a rippled twisted look. It is best used only for curved edges.

Continuous bias binding

1   Cut a square in half diagonally.

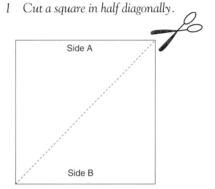

Side A

Side B

2   Align side A and side B right sides together and sew a ¼-inch seam along the edge.

Sides A & B

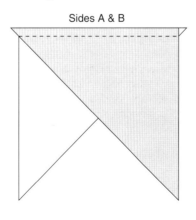

3   Press the seam open. With a long ruler mark 2½-inch strips parallel to the bias edge.

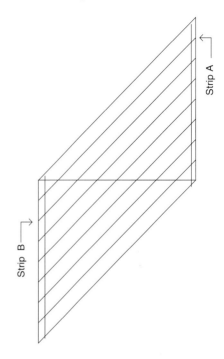

Strip A

Strip B

4   Mark a ¼-inch seam line parallel to the straight grain edges as illustrated.

5   Offset the seam by one strip width joining strip A to strip B. Pin baste at each junction of the marked strips and seam line, and sew along the seam line to form a tube.

6   Start cutting the bias strip at one end, rolling the tube around as you go.

SPEED CUTTING AND PIECING TECHNIQUES

Rotary cutting equipment can greatly speed up the cutting of rectangles and some triangles. It must, however, be used accurately, and it is important to use a consistent seam allowance – ¼ inch is the standard, and is used throughout this book (see page 52). Before cutting, therefore, it helps to recognise and calculate both the finished size and the cut size of a shape. The finished size of a shape does not include the size of the seam allowances. The cut size includes the measurement of the standard ¼-inch seam allowance. The following formulae make it easy to determine the cut dimensions of the most commonly occurring shapes in block patchwork.

Squares

The finished size of a square is determined by the measurement of one of its sides.

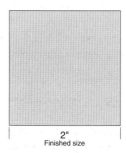

2"
Finished size

The cut size of a square is calculated by adding ½ inch to the finished size.

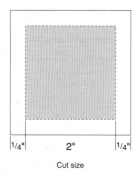

¼"   2"   ¼"
Cut size

Speed cutting squares

For example: to the finished size of a 2-inch square add seam allowances (¼ inch + ¼ inch) or ½ inch for a cut size of 2½ inches.

Speed piecing Four Patch squares

1 Cut one 2½-inch strip of light fabric from selvedge to selvedge, and one of contrasting fabric.
2 Place the fabrics with right sides facing and using a short stitch setting and a ¼-inch seam allowance, join the strips along one long side.

3 Press the closed seam to lock the stitches, then open out and press the seam allowance toward the darker fabric.

4 Using a rotary ruler, straighten the end. Then slice into eight segments 2½ inches wide.

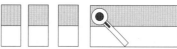

Sew these units together in pairs, with one unit rotated, as illustrated below, to complete the Four Patch unit.

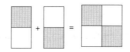

The same principle may be applied to Nine Patch squares, or other combinations.

Half-square triangles

Half-square triangles are obtained by cutting a square in half along one diagonal. The straight grain of the fabric runs parallel to the short sides of the triangle.

The finished size of a half-square triangle is determined by the measurement of one of the short sides.

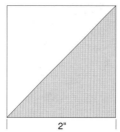

2"

The cut size of a half-square triangle is calculated by adding ⅞ inch to the finished size.

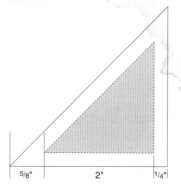

5/8"   2"   ¼"

Speed cutting half-square triangles

1 *For example: to the finished size of a 2-inch half-square triangle add seam allowances (⅝ inch + ¼ inch) or ⅞ inch for a cut size of 2⅞ inch.*
2 *Cut a 2⅞-inch strip of fabric. Slice into 2⅞-inch squares and then slice each square in half along one diagonal to obtain as many half-square triangles as required.*

Speed piecing half-square triangle units

The conventional method for producing half-square triangle units is to cut triangles from each fabric using templates, then to join each unit one by one. However, using the following method it is possible to produce 'ready-sewn' units - the grid facing will yield 12 such units at a time.

The contrasting fabrics are stitched right sides together in a grid pattern, then cut to reveal the units. (Note that the grid may be drafted directly onto the reverse of one of the fabrics, or a paper guide may be made.)

In the illustration (facing page), the solid lines represent cutting lines, and the dotted lines represent sewing lines.

1 *Calculate the cut size of the half-square triangle unit required for your design and on paper draft a 2-square x 3-square master grid to that dimension (the example illustrated is for 2-inch finished units).*
2 *Draw a diagonal line through each*

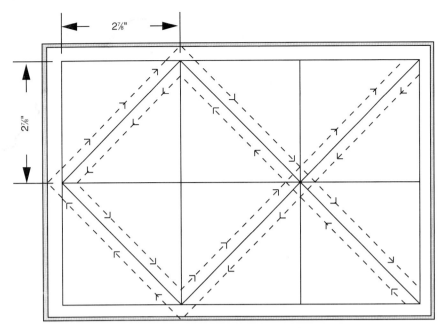

Half-square triangle grid for two-inch finished units

each diagonal. The long side is always on the straight grain.

The finished size of a quarter-square triangle is determined by the measurement of the long side. The cut

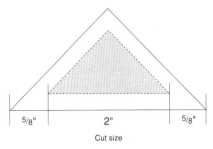

Cut size

size is calculated by adding 1¼ inches to the finished size (see illustration above).

Speed cutting quarter-square triangles

1   *For example: to the finished size of a 2-inch quarter-square triangle add seam allowances (⅝ inch + ⅝ inch, or 1¼ inches) to determine the cut size of the triangle as 3¼ inches. Cut a 3¼-inch strip of fabric.*

2   *Slice into 3¼-inch squares and then slice each square into four across each diagonal*

Speed piecing quarter-square triangle units

As with half-square triangles (see above) there is a very fast method of producing units using a stitched grid. The contrasting fabrics are stitched right sides together in a grid pattern, then cut to reveal the units. The grid below will yield 24 'ready sewn' units. (Note that the grid may be drafted directly onto the reverse of one of the fabrics, or a paper guide may be made.) In the illustration, the solid lines represent cutting lines, and the dotted lines represent sewing lines.

1   *Calculate the cut size of a quarter-square triangle unit required for your design and on paper draft a 2-square x 3-square master grid to this size. Draw diagonal lines in each direction through every square. Sewing lines are drafted ¼ inch to either side of the diagonals running from top left to bottom right*

square as illustrated (solid line). Refer to the illustration and draft a sewing line (dotted line) ¼ inch to either side of each diagonals.

3   *From the two fabrics cut a rectangle slightly larger than the grid size. Copy the grid onto the reverse of one of the fabrics and place them right sides together. Alternatively, make a paper guide: trace off the lines from the master grid onto some tracing or light-weight paper to make a disposable paper guide. Centre the guide on the wrong side of the fabric and secure with some low-tack tape. It helps to stabilise the fabric layers by pinning them together outside the perimeter of the paper guide. Pin to secure, making sure that the pins do not obstruct the sewing line.*

4   *Reduce the machine stitch length slightly and sew the seam exactly on the sewing lines indicated following the direction of the arrows. By pivoting at the corners it is possible to complete the sewing with one seam only.*

5   *Cut into squares first, on the solid lines. Cut into triangles by cutting on the solid lines between the two sewing lines. Peel off the paper guide (if*

used) by folding down and tearing off the seam allowance portion first, supporting the seam firmly between finger and thumb. Press the seams and trim the 'ears' that appear at the

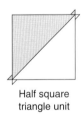

Half square
triangle unit

corner of the squares (see below). Each square of the grid produces two sets of half-square triangle units.

Quarter-square triangle

Quarter-square triangles are obtained by cutting a square into four across

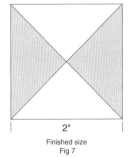

2"

Finished size
Fig 7

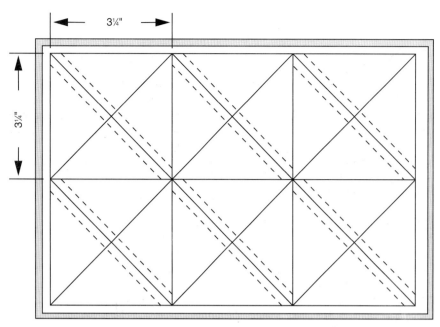

3¼"

3¼"

Quarter-square triangle grid for two-inch finished units

(see illustration above).

2   From the two fabrics cut a rectangle slightly larger than the grid size. Copy the grid onto the reverse of one of the fabrics and place them right sides together. Alternatively, make a paper guide: trace off the lines from the master grid onto some tracing or light-weight paper to make a disposable paper guide. Centre the guide on the wrong side of the fabric and secure with some low-tack tape. It helps to stabilise the fabric layers by pinning them together outside the perimeter of the paper guide. Pin to secure, making sure that the pins do not obstruct the sewing line.

3   Reduce the machine stitch length slightly and sew the seam exactly on the sewing lines indicated. Cut into squares first, along the solid lines, and then cut each square in half between the sewing lines and finally cut the quarter-square triangle  units by cutting on the remaining line. Each square of the grid will produce four pairs of quarter-square triangles which are mirror images of each other.

HINTS FOR SPEED CUTTING AND SEWING TECHNIQUES

● Remember the difference between cut and finished sizes

● Always use an accurate ¼-inch seam allowance

● Keep safety guards on all cutting equipment

● Always use a proper cutting mat

● Use spray starch on floppy fabric to make it easier to handle for cutting

● Keep your sewing machine well oiled and de-fluffed

● Replace burred machine needles immediately

SPECIALIST SUPPLIERS

Candle Makers Supplies
28 Blythe Road, London W14 0HA.
Tel 0171 602 4031.
Shop and mail order: Procion-MX cold water fibre-reactive dyes, fabric paints.

Creative Grids
Leicester Laminating Services,
PO Box 207, Leicester LE3 6YP.
Tel 01162 857 151.
Mail order: template plastic and rotary cutting equipment.

John Lewis Partnership
Department stores: fabrics, fabric paints, cushion pads, fusible linings, wadding and interlinings.

Quilt Basics
2 Meades Lane, Chesham, Bucks HP4 1ND.
Tel 01494 785202.
Mail order: fabrics, patchwork and quilting supplies.

The Quilt Room
Rear Carvilles, Station Road, Dorking, Surrey RH4 1HQ.
Tel 01306 877307.
Mail order: fabrics, patchwork and quilting supplies.

Strawberry Fayre
Chagford, Devon TQ13 8EN.
Tel 01647 433250.
Mail order: fabrics, patchwork and quilting supplies.

George Weil & Sons Limited
Harris Court, 6-5 Riding House Street, London W1P 7PP.
Tel 0171 580 3763.
Shop and mail order: Procion-MX cold water fibre-reactive dyes, fabric paints, cotton and silk fabrics.

PATCHWORK SOCIETIES

National Patchwork Association
PO Box 300, Heathersett, Norwich, Norfolk NR9 3DB.

The Quilters' Guild
OP66, Dean Clough, Halifax, West Yorkshire HX3 5AX.

American Quilters' Society
PO Box 3290 Paducah, KY 42002-3290, USA.

SPECIALIST PUBLICATIONS

From societies:

American Quilter (American Quilters' Society quarterly magazine).

Independent Patchworker (National Patchwork Association quarterly newsletter).

The Quilter (Quilters' Guild quarterly newsletter).

From newsagents:

Patchwork and Quilting (Nexus Media Communications Ltd, bi-monthly magazine).

Popular Patchwork (Traplet Publications, bi-monthly magazine).

US publication:

Quilters Newsletter Magazine (Leman Publications Inc., 10 issues per year).

Thanks to Cara Slattery and my students, who made this series possible. To my husband John for his endless patience, humour and support. To Jaya Adefarasin, Prue Bucknell, Mitsuko Causton, Annette Cole, Mitzi Delnevo, Daisaku Ikeda, Anne Israel, Kim Ritter, Sue Sherriff, Sara Weale, Brenda Woodward and many others for their generosity and encouragement.

ISBN 1 85964 042 7

First edition

British Library Cataloguing-in-Publication Data.
A catalogue record for this book is available from the British Library.

Project management: Jackie Jones
Design: Mark Slader
Photography: Simon Webb
Reprographics: CCTS
Printed in Lebanon

Published by Garnet Publishing Ltd,
8 Southern Court, South Street,
Reading, RG1 4QS, UK

While every care has been taken in the preparation of this book, neither the author nor publishers can accept any liability for any consequences arising from the use of information contained herein.

R54088